COLORADO
BLM WILDLANDS

A Guide To Hiking & Floating Colorado's Canyon Country

By Mark Pearson

Photography by John Fielder

Westcliffe Publishers, Inc.   Englewood, Colordo

Above: Sunset, Squaw/Papoose Canyon Wilderness Study Area
Front Cover Image: Big Dominguez Canyon,
Dominguez Canyon Wilderness Study Area

ACKNOWLEDGMENTS

Recreational use of Colorado's Bureau of Land Management (BLM) lands has grown exponentially in the last 20 years. During this period of booming demand for outdoor recreation, BLM was directed by Congress in 1976 to undertake a thorough evaluation of its roadless lands for wilderness suitability. Conservationists actively participated in BLM's wilderness inventory, even predating BLM's efforts in several cases. This citizen involvement was coordinated by the Colorado Open Space Council (now the Colorado Environmental Coalition — CEC), and one of the tools developed by CEC to better educate and involve the public was a hiking guide to Colorado BLM wildlands: *Finding Freedom: A Guide to Colorado's Unknown Wildlands.*

The guide was published in 1983 by CEC and is now out of print. As one of the original contributors to that guide, I want to thank the editor, Sharyl Kinnear, and the several other contributors, including Norm Mullen, Dick Guadagno and John Stansfield, for their permission to occasionally borrow from *Finding Freedom* in the preparation of this more extensive hiking guide to BLM lands in Colorado.

Many BLM employees also assisted in the preparation of this guide. Although my 13 years of exploration in these areas alone and as a leader of CEC and Sierra Club outings provided me with a solid foundation for preparing the guidebook, my experience was bolstered by conversations with BLM field staff about alternate routes and about legal public access. In particular, Dave Cooper in the Craig District, Carlos Sauvage in Grand Junction and Eric Finstick in the state office gave valuable comments and advice. The many BLM employees who participated in the preparation of the numerous wilderness environmental impact statements and associated planning documents are also to be thanked, for these documents contained a wealth of information and physical data about the areas. Finally, BLM's assistance in obtaining the base maps used for the production of this guide was invaluable.   — MARK PEARSON

International Standard Book Number: 0-929969-86-3
Library of Congress Catalogue Card Number: 91-066711
Copyright:© Mark Pearson, 1992. All rights reserved.
Editor: John Fielder; Copy Editor: Libby Barstow
Production Manger: Mary Jo Lawrence
Typographer: Ruth Koning; Proofreader: Anne R. Higman
Printed in Hong Kong by Twin Age Limited.

Published by Westcliffe Publishers, Inc.
   2650 South Zuni Street, Englewood, Colorado 80110

FOREWORD

My earliest dreams of Colorado conjured views of lofty snowcapped peaks, fields of wildflowers covering the colors of the spectrum, and cool crystalline waters cascading over moss-covered boulders. Those were the dreams of a 13-year-old North Carolinian. As a 21-year-old fresh out of college, I decided to check the accuracy of those dreams. I came to Colorado to seek my fortune.

I may not have found my fortune, at least not right away, but I did learn that my dreams were accurate — almost. Not only did I discover those mountains, flowers and creeks, but ultimately much more. Though the central Rocky Mountains run right through the middle of Colorado, to the east lie the Great Plains of eastern Colorado and to the west the deep canyons of rivers named the Dolores, the Colorado, the Yampa and the Green.

Often overlooked by recreationists, many of these non-mountain places are under the jurisdiction of the Bureau of Land Management (BLM). What most of us have traditionally considered to be boring grazing lands actually are some of Colorado's most scenic areas — and they are virtually undiscovered! Many of these BLM lands are unroaded, affording the hiker or rafter a chance to see Colorado as it existed a thousand years ago, and most are being studied for inclusion in the National Wilderness Preservation System.

In southwestern Colorado, Cross Canyon Wilderness Study Area near the town of Cortez contains many unrestored Anasazi ruins. Whether you seek ancient Indian artwork on rock walls — petroglyphs and pictographs — or just solitude in sweet-smelling piñon-juniper forests, you are guaranteed a unique experience. The Dolores River Canyon Wilderness Study Area hides scenery and wildlife enjoyed by relatively few people.

The BLM wildlands of southwestern Colorado are not unlike those in the midwestern and northwestern sectors of the state. Most are dominated by deep sandstone canyons replete with waterfalls, plunge pools and Indian artifacts. The Grand Junction area offers the world's second greatest accumulation of natural arches, and BLM wildlands in the Craig area contain acclaimed eagle habitat as well as sandstone formations the envy of any sculptor.

In addition, some very special alpine and subalpine mountain lands have slipped through the national forest system. As a result, the BLM manages the columbine wildflowers, black bear and elk that overrun places such as American Flats, Powderhorn and Castle Peak wilderness study areas. Two BLM wildlands actually contain a pair of 14,000-foot peaks — Handies and Redcloud!

When you visit, remember to tread lightly — for Mother Nature is quite fragile, both on high and in desert country. Vehicles are prohibited from entering wilderness study areas by law. Always pack out your trash from the back country, but don't pack out Indian pottery or other antiquities — this is also against the law. Leave things the way they are, so the next person who comes along can imagine they are the first to discover that hidden spot!

Author Mark Pearson has written a marvelous guide — not too much information to spoil the surprises you will encounter, but enough to get you safely in and out. Here are presented 46 of Colorado's most spectacular yet unknown wildlands. I hope you have the opportunity to enjoy them all!

— JOHN FIELDER, Englewood, Colorado

High in a sandstone seep, Dolores River Canyon
Wilderness Study Area. John Fielder photograph.

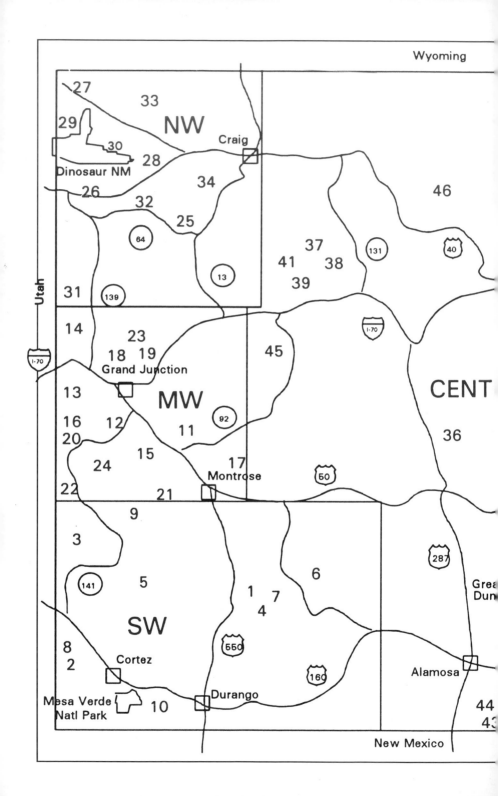

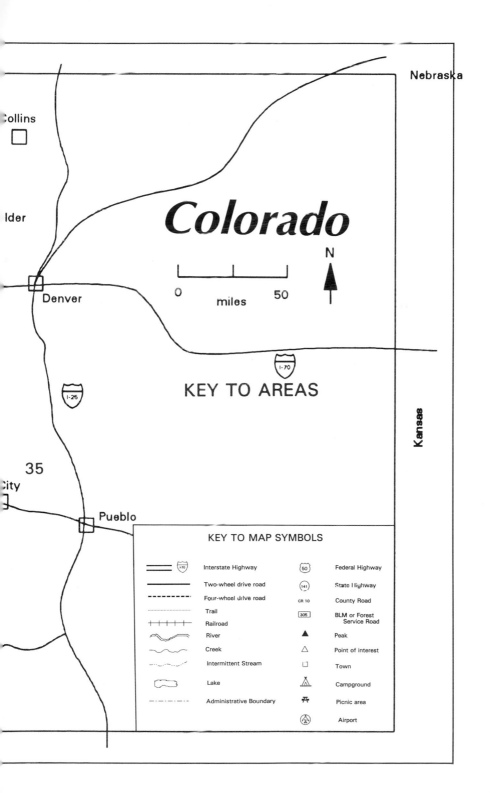

Nebraska

Collins

Ider

Colorado

N

0   miles   50

I-70

KEY TO AREAS

I-26

Kansas

35

City

Pueblo

KEY TO MAP SYMBOLS

═══ I-70	Interstate Highway	(50) Federal Highway
——	Two-wheel drive road	(141) State Highway
– – – –	Four-wheel drive road	CR 10 County Road
··········	Trail	305 BLM or Forest Service Road
+++++++	Railroad	▲ Peak
∿∿	River	△ Point of interest
∼	Creek	⊔ Town
·–··–··	Intermittent Stream	⚏ Campground
⬭	Lake	⊼ Picnic area
– ·· – ·· –	Administrative Boundary	⊛ Airport

TABLE OF CONTENTS

Area Descriptions

PREFACE

The Bureau of Land Management administers more than eight million acres of public lands in Colorado. These lands are often called "the lands no one wanted" because they comprise the public lands that were never disposed of under laws such as the Homestead Act and the Mining Law of 1872, and they were never considered desirable enough for reservation as National Parks or National Forests.

In Colorado, BLM lands are generally found in the western-most third of the state where the Rocky Mountains give way to the arid high mesas and desert canyons of the Colorado Plateau. Other concentrations of BLM land are located in the San Luis Valley and along the Arkansas River between Buena Vista and Pueblo.

BLM lands might be considered the third province of Colorado, the other provinces being the Rocky Mountains and the High Plains. BLM's province is one of desert river canyons, piñon-juniper forests, endangered cactus, America's national symbol — the bald eagle, multicolored badlands, ponderosa pines, innumerable ancient artifacts of long departed Indian cultures, free-roaming wild horse herds and high lonely mesas. In short, these are simply the most unpopulated and remote corners of Colorado and literally the playground of the deer and the antelope.

Colorado's BLM wildlands are "real" wilderness. There are frequently no trails and even fewer trail heads. Signs don't tell you where and where not to tread. Route-finding and orienteering skills are at a premium. In exchange, the visitor is rewarded by a sense of true isolation and exploration, by a longing to see what's around the next bend, over the next knoll, behind the next tree. No tracks and no signs indicate anyone has ever ventured beyond the last roadside, and only relics of bygone eras mark the folly of previous dreamers. There is no coddling, and little handholding, by the benevolent federal stewards of this land. Of course, with these opportunities for a true wilderness experience comes a great deal of responsibility to leave nothing but footprints and very light footprints at that.

All of the areas described in this guidebook have been studied and proposed for designation as wilderness by either BLM (relatively few) or Colorado conservation groups (all of the rest). Wilderness designation means the land would be left in its natural condition for future generations to enjoy and benefit from. No mining, no logging, no road building and no motorized vehicles are allowed to mar areas designated by Congress as wilderness.

BLM lands in Colorado include many ecosystems not currently represented in the National Wilderness Preservation System. In particular, significant downstream portions of most of Colorado's major rivers can be found in these proposed wildernesses. Ruby Canyon on the Colorado River at the Utah state line, Cross Mountain Gorge of the Yampa, 30 miles of the Dolores River above Bedrock, the Gunnison Gorge below the Black Canyon of the Gunnison, Browns Canyon on the Arkansas and the Rio Grande at the New Mexico state line are all described as hikes and floats in this guide.

Of the roughly eight million acres of Colorado BLM lands, hikes are described here for more than one million acres. These million acres represent the land base proposed by Colorado conservationists for wilderness. When combined with adjacent roadless Forest Service lands, the total is almost 1.3 million acres of de facto wildlands. BLM has proposed wilderness protection for approximately 400,000 acres in a lesser number of these areas. Obviously, the areas and hikes described in this guidebook are not a complete list of the recreational opportunities available on Colorado BLM lands. They are, however, the wildest and most natural regions under BLM jurisdiction in Colorado.

Colorado is a state of extraordinary diversity in scenery and ecology. Many of the areas described herein are only a stone's throw off of major state and federal highways, yet they are hidden from the exploring public by a strategically placed hogback or ridge. As you travel the common and remote byways of Colorado, plan your itinerary so you can linger for an afternoon or a weekend at some of these lesser-known hideaways. Many a mesa or slickrock canyon will be revealed with little extra effort.

Because of the generally lower elevation of BLM lands, they are ideal hiking destinations in spring and fall. In springtime, a visitor will often catch the desert at its most glorious wildflower bloom, and in fall many areas lie below popular hunting grounds and thus provide a safe hiking alternative. Other BLM areas form the foothills and transition zones between desert and mountain and are inviting year round.

Anasazi potsherds, Cross Canyon Wilderness Study Area. John Fielder photograph.

INTRODUCTION

How To Use This Guide

For ease of identification, each of the 46 areas in this guide are numbered 1 through 46. Note these reference numbers in the Contents, on the state and regional maps, on regional indexes as well as on the individual area description.

Only a handful of the areas described contain marked and maintained trails. Where trails exist, they have been referenced. In most cases, the area descriptions simply provide directions to canyon mouths or rims and give suggestions about potential hikes from those jumping-off points. The length and rigor of hikes are left largely to the individual hiker.

BLM has divided its administration of public lands in Colorado into four districts, which roughly conform to geographic regions of the state. For example, the Craig District covers northwest Colorado, and the Montrose District covers southwest Colorado. For ease of use, areas are organized in this book by geographic region, beginning in the southwest corner of the state and moving clockwise around Colorado through regions defined as Southwest, Mid-West, Northwest and Central.

Brief information is given at the beginning of each area description so the reader can quickly skim through the area's features. Bullets in these headers give a general sense of location relative to a Colorado town, the area's elevation range, predominant vegetation communities, the amount of roadless country contained in the area, the area's wilderness status, and special features that might be the focus of hikes. The last bullet lists the U.S. Geological Survey (USGS) topographic quadrangles that cover the area described. These USGS quads are the 7.5-minute series unless otherwise specified. USGS maps may be purchased locally from many sporting goods stores or may be ordered directly from the USGS at Western Distribution Branch, USGS, Federal Center, Building 41, P.O. Box 25286, Denver, Colorado 80225.

One other excellent source of maps is Trails Illustrated, P.O. Box 3610, Evergreen, Colorado 80439-3425. Trails Illustrated publishes maps on plastic material that is water and tear resistant. These maps are based on USGS quadrangles and are a particularly heavy duty version for rugged outdoor use.

The BLM series of 1:100,000 surface management maps is an additional source of information that is often invaluable for determining access. These can be obtained from the local BLM office or from well-stocked sporting goods stores. Addresses and phone numbers for all of BLM's resource area offices are listed in Appendix A. Often, local BLM recreation planners can answer questions about routes or give specific advice about road conditions, water availability and other details for trip planning.

Colorado's desert wilderness beckons. Fill your water bottles, grab your pack and boots and head out for one of the purest wilderness experiences you may ever find!

Desert Etiquette

Desert environments are fragile and show the scars of careless or malicious visitors for generations. Desert visitors should carefully follow the admonition to take only pictures and leave only footprints. Even this admonition should be strengthened: Minimize the impact of your footprints. A fragile desert soil cover called cryptogam is often found in remote and unfrequented locations. Cryptogamic soil is characterized by a black, knobby surface that looks like the fungus it partially is. Cryptogams hold the soil together and help to reduce erosion. Hikers' footprints break this cover, leading to increased erosion, so pause to consider your route before plunging ahead through undisturbed mats of cryptogamic soil.

Hike on designated trails where they exist. Frequent cross-country travel may be expected, however; in these areas hikers should use game trails, watercourses, bedrock and other features that reduce the creation of new trails.

Water sources in the desert can be few and far between and are vital to the continued health of native wildlife populations. Be careful not to pollute desert springs, streams and potholes. Camp at least 100 feet from water sources and never wash dishes or bathe in these water sources.

Use a fire pan (stove) instead of building fires. Don't build new fire rings, and in fact you might not need rocks if you build a fire on bare ground. Fires sterilize the soil and blacken rocks, leaving unmistakable evidence of your passage; damage to soil can be reduced by removing the topsoil from your fire pit and then replacing it when finished, eliminating evidence of your fire. In this manner, the soil ecology is disturbed less than with traditional fire rings.

Desert ecosystems have low resistance to trampling and other impacts associated with campsites. Try not to camp in the same location for more than two nights in order to reduce the damage to vegetation and to reduce soil compaction.

Bury human feces six to eight inches deep and burn the toilet paper (if conditions warrant) before filling in the hole.

Be courteous to and considerate of other users of the area. If the area is used for livestock grazing, be sure to close gates behind you and do not harass the livestock.

Pack out whatever you pack in, and try to leave the land without a trace of your visit so the next hikers can imagine themselves as seeing land never before explored.

Don't let the aridity of desert washes and canyons lull you into forgetting that their shape is due to the explosive force of flash floods. Always consider the possibility of unforseen downpours in the surrounding high country as you search for that perfect desert campsite.

One final note. One of the great thrills of hiking in Colorado's western deserts is the chance to encounter remnants of thousand-year-old Anasazi and Fremont civilizations. Not only is it illegal to remove or damage cultural artifacts (such actions are punishable by stiff fines and jail time), but such reckless behavior also destroys an irreplaceable resource for future generations. Please be sure to leave all archaeological sites just as you found them and do not disturb pottery shards, projectile points, corn cobs, structures, petroglyphs or any other type of artifact. Report any suspicious activity at these sites to an appropriate office of BLM.

A Word To Hikers

For the unprepared, the wilderness can be an unforgiving teacher. To ensure the enjoyment of a trip, hikers should possess basic knowledge about wilderness first aid and about appropriate equipment for their adventure. What follows is a brief discussion about environmental exposure and essential equipment that every hiker should keep in mind when exploring wild and remote BLM lands, many of which are far from the beaten track and located where other visitors or BLM management personnel may be few and far between. Numerous books offer more extensive advice about wilderness emergencies, equipment, camping and orienteering skills, food planning, and weather. The Wilderness Education Association and the National Outdoor Leadership School both publish good books about fundamental wilderness skills. Even the most experienced hiker can use an occasional refresher of outdoor survival skills, since the state of knowledge is constantly changing, particularly when it comes to equipment and to wilderness first aid issues such as hypothermia.

Adverse environmental conditions pose the most potentially dangerous situations for outdoor travelers. Extremes of both cold and heat can be encountered in BLM areas in a given season. Wilderness travelers should have a basic understanding of the symptoms of and treatments for the physical reactions to each of these extremes.

Water

Water in the desert is a magical thing. Moisture has a distinctive odor that carries down a canyon, beckoning ever nearer. The fragrance of a moist alcove graced by hanging ferns and a belt of lush greenery is essentially indescribable but certainly unforgettable. Water in many BLM areas is sporadic, transitory and untrustworthy, but when a cool, clear spring is discovered in the midst of the blazing desert heat, it is a treat difficult to overlook.

Much BLM land, however, is situated in sedimentary formations with significant salt content. Alkali-laden streams and springs flowing in these areas are obvious owing to the white rime of salt that adorns their channels, making them look like natural margarita glasses. Hikers might think twice before imbibing from heavily alkaline waters.

Most BLM land is leased for livestock grazing and/or is home to substantial populations of big-game animals. Therefore, hikers should always assume that running water in the desert is home to the parasite *Giardia lamblia* and other microorganisms and should take appropriate precautions. *Giardia lamblia* is a waterborne organism that is transferred via fecal matter from infected animals. Minute cysts that survive for weeks or months in even frigid waters enter a new host and can then cause a disease called giardiasis, which has severe flulike symptoms.

To guard against giardiasis, water of uncertain origin should be treated by boiling, filtering or chemicals. Experts say that *Giardia* cysts are killed by exposure to boiling water at any altitude (it doesn't need to be a hard, rolling boil). Most commonly available water purification filters will also remove the cysts but be sure to check the manufacturer's instructions. Iodine is the only chemical widely recommended for water purification because the effectiveness of chlorine is influenced by water temperature and siltation. Iodine, however, leaves an aftertaste and may need to be camouflaged by flavored drinks.

Sufficient water can usually be carried on day hikes, so only overnight visitors need consider requirements for water purification. Most BLM areas described here have reasonably good sources of water that are easily treated for human use.

Hypothermia

Hypothermia is the lowering of the core body temperature to less than 95° Fahrenheit. Hypothermia can occur in one of two modes: chronic and acute. Chronic hypothermia is the gradual lowering of body temperature over many hours, or even days, and is frequently the result of continued exposure to damp and windy conditions. It can be extremely serious because by the time symptoms appear, a hiker's sources of internal energy have been severely depleted. Two common symptoms characterize chronic hypothermia: exhaustion and lack of coordination. A person experiencing chronic hypothermia will be unable to walk 30 feet in a straight line heel-to-toe. Intense shivering and mild confusion may also occur.

Chronic hypothermia should be treated by preventing further heat loss, primarily by replacing wet clothing with dry clothing, getting out of the wind, and wrapping the victim with numerous layers of insulating clothing. Chronic hypothermia victims are very dehydrated and should be given fluids — preferably warm — to drink. The victim should be warmed by using hot packs (such as hot water in plastic water bottles) applied to the palms and soles or by using the time-honored treatment of cuddling with one or two other hikers in a sleeping bag. Hypothermia victims should be allowed to rest in order to recover needed energy, but if they appear to be slipping deeper into hypothermia they need to be evacuated immediately, since they can slip into a semicomatose state.

Acute hypothermia results from immersion in cold water and occurs within two hours. A good rule of thumb is that anyone who has been immersed in 50°F water for more than 20 minutes is suffering from severe loss of heat. A serious concern with acute hypothermia victims is a phenomenon known as "afterdrop" whereby the victim's core temperature continues to drop even as he or she is being reheated. Because the acute hypothermia victim's skin temperature is so low, substantial amounts of additional heat can be lost simply as blood circulates from the body core to the skin surface. The ideal treatment for an acute hypothermia victim is immersion in hot water (110°F), but a more practical field treatment may be a blazing bonfire. Cuddling in a sleeping bag with one or two bare-skinned rescuers is another means of adding substantial heat to the victim.

Of course, the best cure is prevention. Proper attire, including layering and protection from wind and rain, is a must. Hikers should be in good physical condition, eat food of high nutritional value at regular intervals, and drink plenty of liquids, as much as 16 ounces per hour. Plan your itinerary in a reasonable fashion to prevent exhaustion.

Heat Stress

Most BLM areas are well-described as deserts, and summertime temperatures routinely exceed 100°F. Heat stroke and heat exhaustion are two environmental stresses for which you should be prepared. Heat exhaustion, the less serious of the two, is characterized by the same symptoms as seen for shock. These include a rapid heart rate, pale color, light-headedness, and frequently profuse sweating. Treatment consists of having the victim lie down, elevating the victim's feet, and providing at least one to two quarts of water.

Heat stroke is an extremely serious condition and definitely poses an emergency. In heat stroke, the body has lost its ability to control heating, and the core temperature of the body can rapidly rise to 105°F and even 115°F. Symptoms include red, hot, and dry skin, since the body is unable to cool by sweating. These conditions are life threatening, and the victim's body temperature needs to be immediately reduced. If possible, immerse the victim in cold water, but at a minimum remove the victim to a shaded location. Evaporative cooling in the form of wet clothing can help cool the victim, and massaging the victim's extremities can help circulate blood and further reduce the core temperature. The victim should be evacuated as soon as possible.

Again, prevention is the best medicine. Some hikers suggest wearing light-colored, long-sleeved shirts and long pants made of cotton; others prefer more exposed skin area and sweating to keep cool through evaporation. In either case, drink plenty of water when hiking in hot weather and stop to rest frequently.

Ten Essentials

Many wilderness education organizations teach the idea of "the ten essentials." This is a list of items considered essential for surviving most unexpected events while in the wilderness. One such list consists of the following:

- matches, striker or lighter, and firestarter
- knife
- emergency shelter such as a poncho or ground cloth
- food and water
- first aid kit
- signaling devices such as a mirror or whistle
- map and compass
- sunglasses and sunscreen
- extra clothes
- flashlight with extra batteries and bulb

These items should be carried in your pack at all times, even on the most innocuous seeming hikes, since you never know when the urge might strike to go just a little farther than planned.

A Word To Boaters

Brief descriptions are provided in this guidebook for floating segments of several Colorado rivers. These are by no means intended to provide explicit information about potential hazards or unique conditions of special concern on any given river; instead, they are intended to offer some ideas for trip planning and opportunities for alternative access to the areas. In all cases, it is best to contact the appropriate office of the BLM to obtain specific information about launch sites, features of special interest, and river hazards even though permits are not required for any of the river segments described. BLM has prepared river maps indicating access, mileage, campsites, and land ownership for most of the river segments described. An excellent source for additional information is The *Floater's Guide to Colorado*, by Doug Wheat.

Some of the rivers are described using a common classification scale ranging from easy (Class 1) to unrunnable (Class 6). Several river segments described here contain Class 2 and 3 rapids, significant enough to require scouting rapids before running them.

Most boaters are familiar with the minimum impact camping techniques that are uniformly required on rivers for which permits are issued. It never hurts to review these techniques, however, so accepted practices for reducing or eliminating human impacts to the environment are covered here briefly.

Colorado's rivers all receive substantial use that is increasing yearly. As a result, obvious campsites exist along every river, and it is best to camp in an already impacted site rather than to create significant new resource damage at a pristine site.

Most Colorado rivers transport plenty of debris, so fuel for fires in the form of driftwood is in abundant supply. Please bring a fire pan, however, in which to construct your fire; haul out your ashes with you. Use of a fire pan prevents the blackening of sandy beaches and reduces the negative visual impact of a carpet of charcoal on an otherwise clean beach. A fire pan should have a rim of at least three inches. Soak the ashes thoroughly and scoop any that float into a garbage container. Ashes that sink can be dumped into the main current of the river.

Human waste should similarly be hauled out. A widely used method employs a large rocket box or five-gallon pickle barrel lined with a double layer of heavy duty plastic garbage bags. Odors are reduced by sprinkling lime and chlorine bleach into the bag. When breaking camp, the inner bag is tightly closed with the air squeezed out, a new bag is inserted as the inner liner. On many rivers, BLM provideds a receptacle for human waste at the takeout.

Basic river safety requires a Type III or Type V life jacket for each participant plus one extra jacket per boat. Adequate first aid kits should be included on each boat, along with an extra oar, a repair kit, a rescue throw rope, and a pump.

Certainly there is no substitute for experience. A situation that might seem innocuous to a novice, such as the approach to a bridge piling, can be fraught with danger. Exercise caution and stop to scout any obstacle with which you are unfamiliar.

That said, floating is an exquisite means of exploring much of Colorado's canyon country. The riparian corridors that define these rivers offer a refreshing contrast to the often arid and desolate uplands that surround them. River travel also provides access to secret canyon mouths and many otherwise inaccessible locations. With proper preparation, floating desert rivers can be an unforgettable journey.

WILDERNESS AND THE BLM

The Wilderness Act of 1964 is a rare example of poetry in U.S. legislation. In this extraordinary law, the U.S. Congress expressed its desire that "an increasing population, accompanied by expanding settlement and growing mechanization, does not occupy and modify all areas within the United States" and established the National Wilderness Preservation System. Congress determined that wilderness, "in contrast with those areas where man and his own works dominate the landscape, is hereby recognized as an area where the earth and its community of life are untrammeled by man, where man himself is a visitor who does not remain." Wilderness was further defined as "an area of undeveloped federal land retaining its primeval character and influence, without permanent improvements or human habitation, which is protected and managed so as to preserve its natural condition."

Man's presence in wilderness was recognized, and Congress made allowances for nonimpairing activities to continue within newly designated wilderness areas. Today, human activities allowed within wilderness include non-

Black Rocks and sandstone pinnacles, Ruby Canyon, Black Ridge Canyons Wilderness Study Area. John Fielder photograph.

mechanized recreational activities such as hiking, horse packing, floating, hunting and fishing as well as livestock grazing, fire suppression, treatment of insect infestations and diseases and maintenance of existing water diversion facilities. Activities deemed incompatible with the purposes of wilderness include mining, logging, road construction and use of mechanized equipment such as motor vehicles, snowmobiles, chain saws, bicycles and hang gliders.

The National Park Service and the U.S. Forest Service, but not the Bureau of Land Management, were directed by the original Wilderness Act to undertake studies of lands under their jurisdiction and make recommendations to Congress about which lands should be placed in the National Wilderness Preservation System. Congress reserved the final decision as to the designation of wilderness areas to itself.

In Colorado, both the National Park Service and the U.S. Forest Service completed the required wilderness studies and reports throughout the 1970s. Congress acted on many of these recommendations, so that by 1981 approximately 2.6 million acres of federal wilderness had been designated in National Parks and National Forests. The designations covered many of Colorado's most significant wildland resources. Only five areas had been designated with the enactment of the original 1964 Act — Rawah, Mount Zirkel, Maroon Bells, West Elks and La Garita. The Weminuche and Flat Tops wildernesses were designated in 1975, Eagles Nest in 1976 and Indian Peaks and Hunter-Fryingpan in 1978. The majority of Colorado wilderness was set aside in 1980 legislation with the culmination of the Forest Service Roadless Area Review and Evaluation II. The 2.6 million acres of wilderness thus designated, however, amount to only 4 percent of Colorado's 66-million-acre land base.

During this era, Congress and the public came to recognize the importance of desert wild country under the administration of the BLM, and in 1976 Congress passed the Federal Land Policy and Management Act (FLPMA) that for the first time placed BLM on equal footing with the Forest Service. In FLPMA, Congress stated that it was the policy of the United States to retain ownership of the hundreds of millions of acres of BLM public lands throughout the West and directed BLM to conduct a thorough review of its lands and make recommendations about the wilderness suitability of those lands to Congress by 1993.

In Colorado, BLM initially determined that approximately 1.2 million acres of its eight million acres were largely roadless. The Wilderness Act defines wilderness as an area with outstanding opportunities for solitude or primitive and unconfined recreation. In applying this definition, BLM decided that although one-third of the roadless lands did have some opportunity for solitude and primitive recreation, those opportunities were not of an outstanding nature. As a result, only 800,000 acres were identified as Wilderness Study Areas by BLM in 1980.

Since 1980, BLM field offices around Colorado have conducted exhaustive reviews of these potential wilderness areas, and after considering alternative uses for them such as mining and water projects, BLM has proposed approximately 400,000 acres, or 5 percent of BLM land in Colorado, for designation as wilderness. Colorado BLM officials forwarded their recommendations to the president in October 1991, and as of this edition (Spring 1992), President

Bush had not yet presented those recommendations to Congress for its consideration. Wilderness designations are typically considered on a state-by-state basis by Congress, so it is now up to the Colorado congressional delegation to prepare legislation that reflects the desires of both the BLM and the public users of BLM wildlands.

Colorado conservation groups conducted field studies separately from BLM. Determining the "outstanding" nature of solitude is obviously a subjective procedure, so in many cases conservation groups proposed areas for wilderness that BLM had earlier discarded for lack of outstanding solitude or primitive recreation. These areas are included in this guidebook, and you the reader will be in the best position to influence the final decision on the fate of these areas. BLM lands proposed for wilderness by Colorado conservation groups total more than one million acres. Many of these BLM areas are adjacent to roadless Forest Service lands, so when another 300,000 acres of Forest Service wildlands are included, the conservation groups' proposal amounts to about 1.3 million acres. As Congress weighs the relative merits of the BLM and conservation group proposals for BLM wilderness areas, it will actively solicit input from citizens. If you would like more information about Colorado conservation groups that are active in issues affecting BLM wilderness lands, refer to Appendix B for addresses and phone numbers.

Wilderness Issues

Designation of federal lands as wilderness stirs strong passions among affected interest groups. Conservation groups advocate protection of wilderness areas for many reasons. These include the necessity for unmodified ecological baseline areas to serve as early warning indicators of wholesale environmental changes, a desire to preserve a representative sample of the historic landscape, and the creation of genetic repositories to replenish weakened species and ecosystems in developed regions. Other reasons are to protect scientific warehouses of undiscovered species and flora and fauna with as yet unknown medicinal or utilitarian values, to preserve landscapes with extraordinary aesthetic qualities and to maintain recreational opportunities that challenge the most-skilled outdoors lovers.

Wilderness designation frequently runs headlong into commercial interests that have traditionally used public lands for a variety of purposes, most prominently logging, livestock forage, mining and water development. People with other interests, such as motorized recreationists, object to the preservation of selected areas as wilderness because their recreational activity is excluded. There will be few if any conflicts between wilderness designation of BLM lands and logging simply because most BLM areas are located in semiarid regions and lack commercial timber resources. The potential for conflicts between other uses and wilderness does exist, however, and deserves some elaboration.

Grazing

The Wilderness Act specifically allows for livestock grazing to continue in the same manner and degree as was occurring at the time an area was designated wilderness. Congress has gone beyond this legislative language in committee reports to explicitly direct federal agencies that there be "no curtailments of grazing in wilderness areas simply because an area is, or has been, designated wilderness, nor should wilderness designations be used as an excuse by administrators to slowly 'phase out' grazing." Ranchers are even allowed exceptions to the general wilderness prohibition against motorized vehicles in wilderness, as long as the use of the vehicles is infrequent and only for required repairs to range improvements like fences and stock tanks or for emergencies. In addition, ranchers are permitted to construct new range improvements and replace deteriorated facilities as needed to prevent damage to natural resources.

It is apparent from this congressional direction that wilderness designation and continued livestock grazing are compatible. It is the opinion of most conservation organizations that the federal agencies responsible for the administration of grazing in wilderness areas have implemented this direction in a manner that has done little to impair wilderness qualities. Many livestock operators also apparently have little quarrel with the existing application of these guidelines. In testimony on several bills concerning Colorado National Forest wilderness additions in 1984, a representative of the Colorado Cattlemen's Association praised this system and noted the lack of problems between livestock operators and the Forest Service.

Still, individual ranchers and agricultural groups frequently oppose wilderness designations simply because they view wilderness as potentially imposing additional regulation on their commercial use of public lands. These objections are more deeply rooted in ideology than they are in fact.

Mining

The Wilderness Act states that "the minerals in lands designated by this Act as wilderness areas are withdrawn from all forms of appropriation under the mining laws and from disposition under all laws pertaining to mineral leasing." Only mineral rights established prior to the wilderness designation, or prior to BLM's identification of an area as a Wilderness Study Area, can be developed.

This outright prohibition of mining in wilderness commonly creates a perceived conflict with wilderness designation. Most of the perceived conflicts on BLM lands arise from energy minerals, such as oil, natural gas and coal. Hard-rock minerals like gold and silver pose few conflicts with most BLM wilderness proposals, since the majority of the proposed areas are in sedimentary rock formations that are poor source rocks for hard-rock minerals. There are a few exceptions, however, in mountainous regions like the San Juans where BLM administers several 14,000-foot peaks.

Because few of the proposed BLM wilderness areas lie in either of the two most significant BLM coal-producing regions in Colorado — the North Fork of the Gunnison valley and the Craig-Hayden area — there are few conflicts with coal mining. One or two areas in the Book Cliffs near Grand Junction contain quantities of low-quality coal, but the Book Cliffs are a minor coal-producing region. BLM's Resource Management Plans report approximately 25 billion tons of recoverable coal reserves on over 1.6 million acres of federal lands in Colorado. In contrast, the proposed wilderness areas cover only 0.7

billion tons of these potential coal reserves on 50,000 acres. The proposed wilderness areas thus include a scant three percent of recoverable coal reserves in Colorado, none of which are in the state's prime coal producing regions.

According to BLM's Resource Management Plans and Umbrella Oil and Gas Leasing Environmental Assessments, almost eight million acres of BLM-administered mineral lands in Colorado are open to oil and gas leasing. The wilderness acreage proposed by conservation groups is equal to about 13 percent of the BLM acreage open to leasing. Much of the proposed wilderness has been leased at some time or another but was not extensively explored because of lack of interest by the leaseholders. Despite this record, oil and gas development is likely to be the greatest land-use conflict with potential wilderness designations on BLM lands.

There are no recoverable oil shale resources within any of the proposed wilderness areas simply because there are no roadless areas left in the Piceance Basin that qualify for wilderness protection.

Water

As with other federally reserved lands, wilderness areas are entitled to federal water rights sufficient for the purposes of the designation of the wilderness. The purposes of a wilderness designation in most cases include recreation, protection of fish and wildlife habitat, aesthetic values and maintenance of riparian ecosystems, among others. The concept of reserved water rights dates to a U.S. Supreme Court decision in 1908 concerning an Indian reservation in Montana. In that case, the court ruled that it made little sense to reserve land for a specific purpose (in this case for the resettlement of an Indian tribe) if enough water was not also reserved to meet the purposes of the reservation. The court later expanded the reserved rights doctrine to include any federal reservation, including National Parks and National Forests. Conservation groups argue that wilderness, as yet another form of congressional reservation, is similarly entitled to enough water to satisfy its purposes.

Wilderness water rights are adjudicated in state water court pursuant to Colorado water law. The priority date for wilderness water rights is the date of wilderness designation of the area; thus no wilderness area can have a water right more senior than 1964. According to BLM, there are few significant conflicts between wilderness designation and private water rights. In a synopsis of potential water rights conflicts with BLM wilderness prepared by BLM for Congressman George Miller on August 19, 1988, the BLM stated that it expected in-depth analysis of the issue "will probably demonstrate that the real impacts are small and easily mitigated."

A major reason for the lack of conflicts is that the majority of proposed BLM wilderness areas are headwaters areas; that is, the areas are situated at the heads of watersheds with the result that no water flows into the areas from outside their boundaries. Other areas that might be considered nonheadwaters areas (areas into which streams flow) are downstream only from designated wilderness or other protected areas, thus posing no potential conflict with any upstream water user. BLM wilderness areas will carry very junior priority water rights, so preexisting water uses will not be affected by BLM wilderness water rights because of seniority.

It is also important to note that since the proposed wilderness areas are largely in desert regions, watercourses that flow into nonheadwaters areas are generally ephemeral in nature, with limited or nonexistent opportunities for upstream diversion. There are, however, several areas situated on major rivers such as the Dolores, Gunnison and Yampa.

Many water users in Colorado object to the concept of federal reserved water rights due to a fear of federal government intervention in what has traditionally been a state arena, despite the fact that all water rights are adjudicated in state water courts. Water users believe that if downstream wilderness areas on major rivers are granted even a very junior water right, the presence of that right could reduce the opportunities for development of new upstream water rights or could prevent some types of changes in use of existing water rights.

Substantial conflicts with water rights may occur where there is or has been proposed a reservoir site that would inundate portions of the proposed wilderness. These instances include major on-stream reservoirs proposed for the Gunnison and Yampa rivers, but most observers believe the chances are extremely remote that billion-dollar dams will ever be built on these rivers, and therefore the possibility of any real conflict is minimal.

Recreation

As mentioned above, wilderness possesses far more values, and perhaps more important values, for civilization than simply to exist as a setting for primitive recreational pursuits such as backpacking and horse packing. Motorized recreationists, however, often see wilderness designation as a conflict between categories of recreational users, and all too often wilderness debates are reduced to trading charges of recreational elitism. The recreational value of wilderness lies in the opportunity to ensure that undisturbed landscapes will always exist for human exploration and challenge. Primitive types of recreation occur largely in wilderness simply because wilderness areas are the only fragments of North America still possessing wild character. Literally millions of acres are available for nonwilderness forms of recreation, on lands that will never be suitable for protection as wilderness. It seems unproductive to argue about the recreational use of shrinking wildlands when ample alternatives exist for nonwilderness-dependent forms of recreation like off-road vehicles.

Off-road vehicles come in many shapes and sizes, including four-wheel-drive vehicles, motorcycles, all-terrain vehicles and snowmobiles. The authors of the Wilderness Act prohibited these machines from designated wilderness under the belief that such obvious signs of civilization and their accompanying noise and potential for environmental damage were incompatible with the objectives of wilderness areas.

Bicycles were similarly prohibited because they represent a mechanical advantage and were deemed inappropriate in wilderness. Machines such as bicycles effectively shrink the wilderness, allowing a visitor to cover distances in a short time that might otherwise require several days of foot travel. The spirit of wilderness is one of shedding the trappings and pace of civilization in favor of the slower rhythms found in nature.

SOUTHWEST COLORADO

Opposite: Anasazi tower, Ruin Canyon, Cross Canyon Wilderness Study Area. John Fielder photograph.

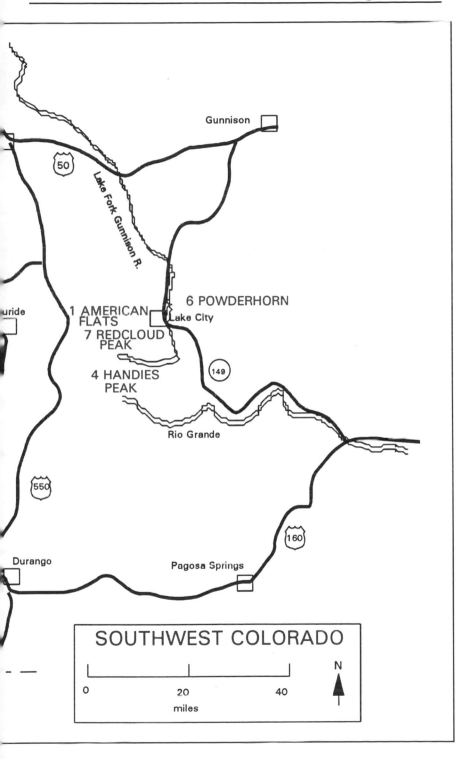

SOUTHWEST COLORADO

John Fielder

1   AMERICAN FLATS

Location:	17 miles west of Lake City
Elevation Range:	11,000 – 13,000 feet
Vegetation/Ecosystem:	Spruce-fir; alpine tundra
Roadless Acreage:	3,065 acres
Wilderness Status:	1,505 acres proposed for wilderness by BLM
Special Features:	American Lake; tundra; rugged peaks
USGS Maps:	Handies Peak, Uncompahgre Peak, Wetterhorn Peak

American Flats is aptly named for the gentle expanse of rolling tundra north of Engineer Pass. Its alpine tundra sits amid breathtaking 13,000- and 14,000-foot peaks of the San Juan Mountains and includes 13,266-foot Wildhorse Peak. American Flats is adjacent to the Forest Service Big Blue Wilderness and encompasses the headwaters of Wildhorse Creek and Cow Creek, which flow northward into the wilderness. The flats afford unrestricted views of nearby Wetterhorn and Uncompahgre peaks, two fourteeners (as Colorado's

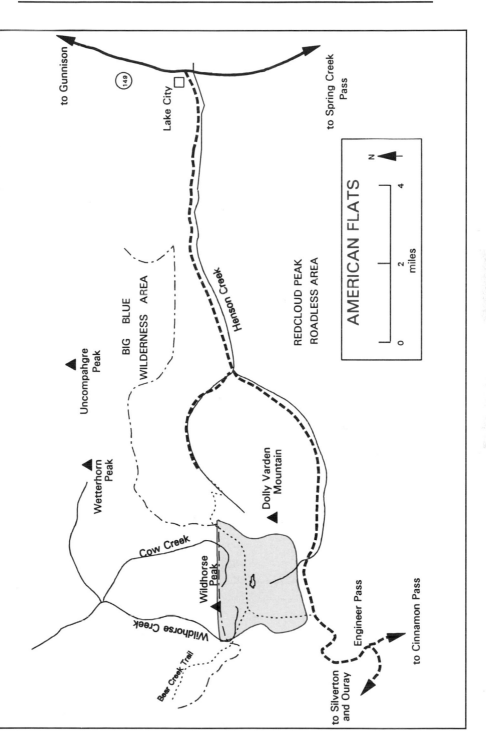

AMERICAN FLATS

14,000-foot peaks are called) that rise sharply above the high alpine plain. American Flats also includes American Lake, a small alpine lake perched at the head of Henson Creek.

American Flats is easily accessible from the popular Engineer Pass Road. An abandoned vehicle track that is now only two fading ruts across the tundra leads directly across the flats and circles east to American Lake. This track leaves the Engineer Pass road approximately 2.5 miles beyond its fork with Schafer Gulch, immediately east of the rugged ridge that forms the Hinsdale-Ouray county line, and is marked by a BLM sign prohibiting vehicles. Some of the easiest alpine hiking in all of Colorado is found along this route; the gentle to nonexistent grade is particularly suited for elderly or infirm hikers who wish to venture amid the dazzling summer displays of alpine wildflowers. There is interest here for the historically minded as well. Members of the Hayden Survey in 1874 crossed the plateau of American Flats to its western edge, whence they studied the possibilities of climbing Mount Sneffels.

American Flats can also be reached from the west via the Bear Creek or Horse Thief trails from Ouray and the Red Mountain Pass highway.

John Fielder

2   CROSS CANYON

Location:	25 miles northwest of Cortez
Elevation Range:	5,000 – 6,600 feet
Vegetation/Ecosystem:	Cottonwoods; sagebrush; piñon-juniper
Roadless Acreage:	23,262 acres
Wilderness Status:	Not proposed for wilderness by BLM
Special Features:	Numerous archaeological sites; desert riparian zone
USGS Maps:	Cahone, Cajon Mesa (15'), Champagne Spring, Monument Canyon (15'), Negro Canyon, Ruin Canyon

Cross Canyon and its tributaries, Cahone Canyon, Cow Canyon and Ruin Canyon, drop abruptly from surrounding mesas into 300- to 900-foot-deep canyons. The area includes almost 30 twisting miles of Cross Canyon and

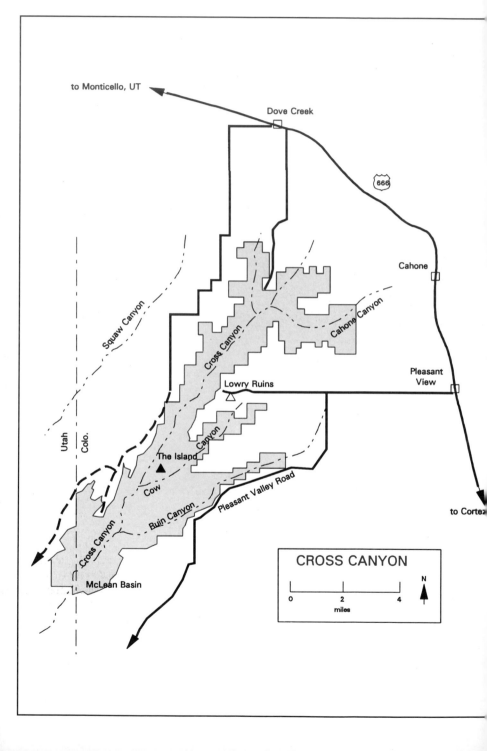

to Monticello, UT

Dove Creek

666

Cahone

Squaw Canyon

Cross Canyon

Cahone Canyon

Lowry Ruins

Pleasant View

Utah

Colo.

Canyon

The Island

Cow

Ruin Canyon

Pleasant Valley Road

to Cortez

Cross Canyon

McLean Basin

CROSS CANYON

0   2   4
miles

N

more than 25 miles of tributaries. The canyon bottoms are lined with cottonwood trees fed by streams with some inviting pools and waterfalls.

The native piñon-juniper forests which dominate the upland mesas surrounding Cross Canyon have seen extensive development by agriculture, and by exploration for oil, gas and carbon dioxide. However, the canyon slopes are covered with numerous shrubs such as mountain-mahogany, serviceberry and rabbitbrush in addition to the prevalent piñon-juniper. Mule deer, mountain lions, and even an occasional black bear can be found in the canyon as well as raptors including golden and bald eagles and peregrine falcons.

The long riparian canyons not only provide a haven for wildlife but also were a source of sustenance for Anasazi (ancient Indians) who lived there between A.D.450 and 1300. The ruins and artifacts left in this area are literally everywhere, in concentrations of 40 to 60 (and even 100) sites per square mile, making it a denser collection of cultural resources than anywhere else in the United States. Kivas and small storage structures are hidden among the rocks and cliffs, and an intact square tower similar to those at Hovenweep National Monument may be found in Ruin Canyon. It is easy to find rock art on the canyon walls and frequent pieces of pottery in the dirt, but please don't deface or remove these traces of ancient cultures.

The easiest access into the roadless area is from BLM's Lowry Ruins National Historic Site. Follow the signs to the ruins approximately nine miles west from the hamlet of Pleasant View on Highway 160. The ruins sit at the head of Cow Canyon on the boundary of the roadless area. From the parking lot at the ruins, head south down the drainage into Cow Canyon. The canyon intersects with Cross Canyon in about eight miles. For an overnight trip, hike up Cross Canyon five or six miles and then strike out cross-country south and west back to Cow Canyon near Lowry Ruins.

Aptly named Ruin Canyon is another long tributary of Cross Canyon. Head west from Pleasant View and turn south at 5.5 miles along the Pleasant Valley Road. This road heads west to the rim of Ruin Canyon in three miles and generally parallels the canyon for about five miles. You can park where the road crosses public land and drop into the canyon, or you can head west on a lower-quality road that becomes more and more primitive as you drop into McLean Basin. A cylindrical tower ruin has been fenced off in McLean Basin by BLM and other ruins are obvious in Ruin Canyon. One-day and multiday loop trips are possible through Ruin, Cross, and Cow canyons. The connecting leg between Ruin and Cow canyons requires a couple of miles of cross-country hiking through piñon-juniper forests across the intervening mesa.

From the east end of Dove Creek, drive due south from Highway 160 to the end of the road in approximately nine miles to access Cross Canyon and Cahone Canyon from the north. The road ends at an old drill pad above the confluence of Cross, Cahone and Dove creeks. Scramble down the shallow canyon slopes into Cross Canyon, and either hike downstream or take one of the branches up Cahone Canyon or Dove Creek. Private land on the intervening mesas precludes loop trips between these canyons.

The perennial streams in the Cross Canyon roadless area are largely fed by agricultural runoff and may be of dubious water quality.

John Fielder

3   DOLORES RIVER CANYON

Location:	17 miles west of Naturita
Elevation Range:	5,000 – 6,600 feet
Vegetation/Ecosystem:	Boxelder-tamarisk; sagebrush; piñon-juniper
Roadless Acreage:	33,480 acres
Wilderness Status:	29,415 acres proposed for wilderness by BLM
Special Features:	Dolores River; slickrock canyons; scenic vistas; petroglyphs
USGS Maps:	Anderson Mesa, Bull Canyon, Davis Mesa, La Sal (15'), Lisbon Valley (15'), Paradox

Dolores River Canyon is a pristine desert canyonland containing some of the most outstanding canyon scenery in Colorado. The area includes a segment of the Dolores River recommended as a wild river under the Wild and Scenic Rivers Act, surrounding benchlands and mesa uplands and portions of five

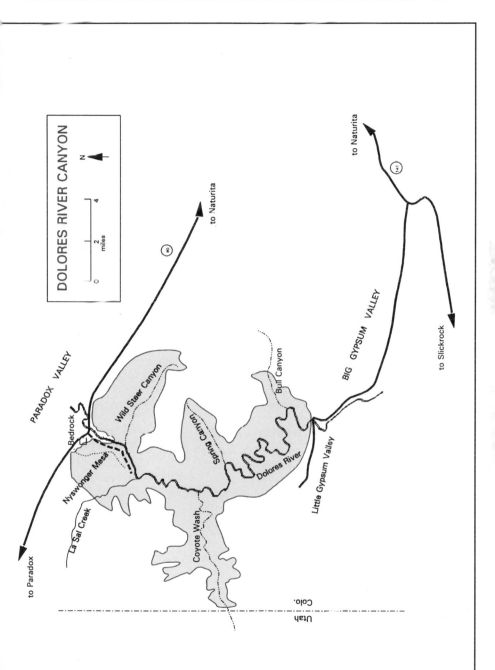

major tributary canyons. Twelve geological formations are exposed by the river in the gorge — the predominant formation being the spectacular cliff-forming red Wingate Sandstone. The cliffs rise to benches of bedrock 500 to 700 feet above the river, with the canyon rim 1,100 feet above the river. The tributary canyons include La Sal Creek — a deep and twisting canyon cut by a perennial stream — Coyote Wash, Spring Canyon, Bull Canyon and Wild Steer Canyon, all delightful canyons with sculpted slickrock and plunge pools.

Dolores River Canyon is home to a variety of wildlife, including the en-dangered peregrine falcon known to be nesting in Paradox Valley and believed to be hunting in the Dolores River Canyon area. Mule deer, mountain lions and bobcats are common inhabitants of the area; golden eagles nest here and hunt, as do bald eagles. Dolores River Canyon is also home to reintroduced populations of bighorn sheep and river otters.

Vegetation varies from piñon-juniper woodland, oakbrush and sagebrush on the mesa uplands to riparian species of plants along the river, including tamarisk, willows, boxelder, rushes, sedges and occasional cottonwoods. A number of rare plants grow within the area, including the Eastwood monkey-flower (said to grow in shallow caverns in cliffs on the lower portion of Coyote Wash), kachina daisy and *Mertensia arizonica*.

This stretch of the Dolores River is very popular for rafting, kayaking and canoeing. The rafting season usually occurs during late May and early June, and there are several Class II rapids in the canyon, though since McPhee Dam was completed upstream there has frequently been insufficient spring runoff to support a boating season. Boaters launch at Slickrock or Little Gypsum Valley off of Highway 141, and the takeout is at Bedrock in the Paradox Valley on Highway 90. Hiking is popular in the tributary canyons, with Coyote Wash a favorite stopping place for rafters to walk barefoot in the sandy streambed. Several petroglyphs are found in the tributary canyons and in the main gorge. Bull Canyon includes a cold plunge pool, and Spring Creek has a wide, slickrock bottom with several low alcoves.

La Sal Creek is accessible either by boat or overland from Bedrock. To hike into La Sal Creek, park at the Bedrock boat ramp and follow the four-wheel-drive trail along the west bank of the river three miles to the mouth of La Sal Creek. La Sal Creek is perhaps the largest creek draining the La Sal Mountains, but water quality may be suspect due to agricultural practices upstream and a metals mine just outside the roadless area boundary, approximately three miles upstream. Ambitious hikers can proceed farther up the Dolores beyond the mouth of La Sal Creek, particularly in summer and fall when the water level is frequently only 20 cubic feet per second (cfs).

A hike across Nyswanger Mesa affords absolutely stunning views of the surrounding snowcapped peaks of the La Sals and San Juans. An abandoned four-wheel-drive trail, now impassable to vehicles, heads up the cliffs less than a mile west of Bedrock. Park along Highway 90 and follow this trail across the mesa. A network of bladed ways, relics from wantonly destructive uranium exploration, crisscrosses the piñon-juniper forests and sagebrush meadows of the mesa but creates a relatively small impact on its overall naturalness. In about three miles you will reach the southern point of the mesa and look straight down into the Dolores River Canyon and La Sal Creek. From this vantage point, La Sal Creek and its tributaries carve a wild labyrinth through glaring white sandstone cliffs, set off by a green mat of piñon-juniper and highlighted by the snowcapped La Sal Mountains.

Sunrise, Dolores River Canyon Wilderness Study Area. John Fielder photograph.

4   HANDIES PEAK

Location:	15 miles southwest of Lake City
Elevation Range:	9,500 – 14,048 feet
Vegetation/Ecosystem:	Spruce-fir; tundra
Roadless Acreage:	63,000 acres (includes 45,000 acres of Forest Service Land)
Wilderness Status:	7,120 acres proposed for wilderness by BLM*
Special Features:	14,048 Handies Peak; Continental Divide; glacial valleys; alpine lakes
USGS Maps:	Finger Mesa, Handies Peak, Howardsville, Lake San Cristobal, Pole Creek Mountain, Redcloud Peak

*BLM's favorable wilderness recommendation for Handies Peak was vetoed by Interior Secretary Manuel Lujan in September 1991.

Handies Peak, when combined with Carson Peak on adjacent National Forest lands, is one of the largest unprotected roadless areas remaining in Colorado. The area contains 15 miles of the Continental Divide in the midst of the exceptionally scenic San Juan Mountains, sitting at the headwaters of both the Rio Grande and of the Lake Fork of the Gunnison River. Handies Peak (14,048 feet) is the most prominent feature in the northern end of the area, and two 13,700-foot peaks, Carson Peak and Pole Creek Mountain, dominate the expansive tundra to the south. Handies Peak is the fortieth highest peak in Colorado and the highest peak under BLM jurisdiction outside of Alaska.

The landforms of this area present intriguing contrasts. The Lake Fork side is precipitous and rugged, characterized by massive volcanic peaks and huge glaciated valleys and is dotted with numerous waterfalls and moss-covered grottoes. These valleys provide access to the high rolling tundra and volcanic peaks of the central part of the area. Deep valleys drain south into the Rio Grande. A particularly unique feature of these southerly drainages is the presence of volcanic "beehives" — cones of ash and lava — some of which sit astride Pole Creek in the form of arches.

To reach Handies Peak, head south from Lake City past Lake San Cristobal toward Cinnamon Pass. The roadless area begins just west of the Wager Gulch four-wheel-drive trail and includes the almost vertical valley walls south of Mill Creek Campground.

To climb Handies Peak, follow the Lake Fork to its source high in American Basin. Hike into the basin toward Sloan Lake and simply climb east to the saddle and onto the peak. A longer, less-traveled route begins at the mouth

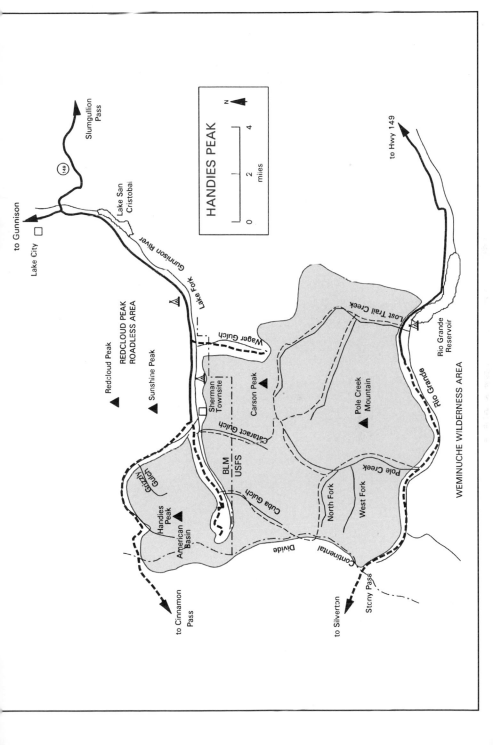

Handies Peak from Grizzly Gulch, Handies Peak Wilderness Study
Area. John Fielder photograph.

of Grizzly Gulch northeast of the peak. A steep trail heads up the valley. As the trail breaks out above timberline, angle toward the north ridge and onto the summit. This route also leads to Whitecross Mountain, north along the same ridge.

The larger Forest Service section of the roadless area offers many miles of absolutely gorgeous alpine hiking, including 12 miles of the Colorado Trail and the Continental Divide Trail. Two magnificent hanging glacial valleys, Cuba Gulch and Cataract Gulch, lead south into the heart of the Carson Peak area. A rough four-wheel-drive trail leads to the Cuba Gulch trail along Cottonwood Creek about five miles west of Sherman. The Cuba Gulch trail passes several sparkling cascades and quickly breaks out above timberline into a wide valley filled with willows and other alpine vegetation. In about seven miles you reach the Continental Divide, from which you can travel south to trails in the North and West forks of Pole Creek. Both forks lead to Pole Creek and the Colorado Trail.

The Cataract Gulch trail leads more directly to Pole Creek. Beginning just a mile west of Sherman, the trail crosses Cottonwood Creek, switchbacks into the hanging glacial valley and reaches Cataract Lake in several miles. From Cataract Lake you can connect with the Pole Creek Trail or head east along the Colorado Trail. Half Peak, just west of the lake, is an interesting and very scenic climb.

John Fielder

5   MCKENNA PEAK

Location:	25 miles south of Naturita
Elevation Range:	6,300 – 8,800 feet
Vegetation/Ecosystem:	Piñon-juniper; Douglas-fir; ponderosa pine
Roadless Acreage:	21,080 acres
Wilderness Status:	Not proposed for wilderness by BLM
Special Features:	Shale badlands; sandstone buttes; fossils; wild horses
USGS Maps:	Glade Mountain, McKenna Peak, North Mountain, South Mountain

McKenna Peak possesses a diversity of values that include a rich fossil resource of clams and brachiopods from the Cretaceous era (100 million years ago), a diverse range of vegetative communities from grassland to coniferous forests, an established herd of wild horses and scenic, eroded adobe badlands presided over by imposing sandstone cliffs rising 2,000 feet above the plain.

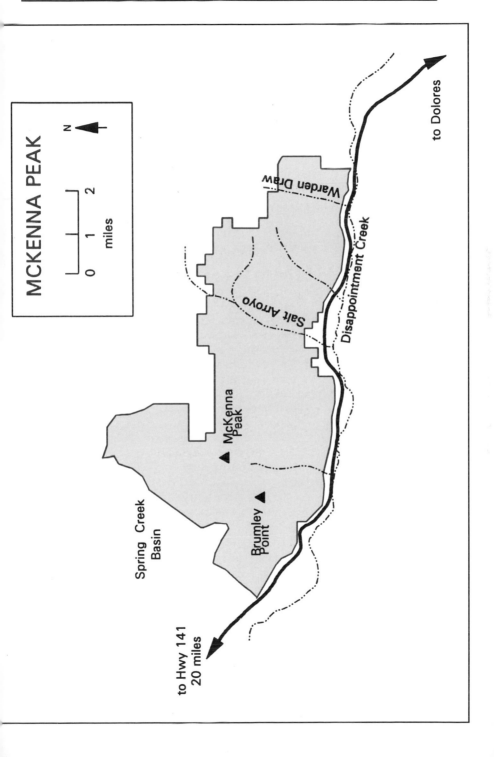

The McKenna Peak roadless area ranges in elevation from 6,300 to 8,800 feet. The lower-elevation western and southern portions of the area comprise gentle, barren shale flats broken by occasional mesas and buttes of eroded shale highlands. McKenna Peak itself is a highly symmetrical, barren, gray-colored cone with radiating ridge spines and gullies. Vegetation here is sparse, consisting of scattered grasses and colorful wildflowers, with widely separated piñons and junipers lining the ridges. You can hike to the top of 8,400-foot McKenna Peak from the Disappointment Valley Road, which heads east from Highway 141 between Slickrock and Gypsum Gap. Follow the Disappointment Valley Road approximately 25 miles southeast to a winding badland gully that heads straight north toward McKenna Peak. Take the gully to the base of McKenna Peak and then simply scramble up any of the symmetrical slopes of the peak.

An impressive ridge of sandstone cliffs forms a towering backdrop rising 2,000 feet above the shale badlands. Lush forests of ponderosa pine and Douglas-fir exist atop these cliffs, providing refreshingly cool refuges in summer from the oven-furnace heat of the lower badlands. These forests include extremely important winter wildlife habitat for large numbers of deer and elk in the area bordering North Mountain, now considered to have one of the largest deer and elk herds in all of Colorado. The wild horse herd numbers about 100 and roams the western reaches of the area in the Spring Creek Basin. A very rocky four-wheel-drive trail heads into the basin from the Disappointment Valley road. Bald eagles winter in the lower reaches of the area and peregrine falcons have been sighted in the area as well. Mountain lions, bobcats and black bear are also known to inhabit McKenna Peak.

Scaling one of the huge sandstone cliffs results in a particularly outstanding sense of isolation as you peer into the yawning spaciousness of the unfolding badlands below. The butte west of Warden Draw offers one such opportunity. At the east end of the roadless area, park along a four-wheel-drive trail in the mouth of Warden Draw and hike north a short distance until a route up the steep, soft slopes of the butte becomes apparent through the forest. A slot in the rim sandstone provides the final route to the top. Once through the bright yellow sandstone rim, hikers are rewarded by the cool shade of Douglas-fir trees that populate the protected north and west slopes of the butte. There are few contrasts so substantial as surveying shimmering heat waves radiating off of shale badlands from a cool retreat such as that provided by a Douglas-fir forest high above the desert.

6   POWDERHORN

Location:	Five miles northeast of Lake City
Elevation Range:	8,600 – 12,600 feet
Vegetation/Ecosystem:	Sagebrush-grasslands; ponderosa pine; spruce-fir; alpine tundra
Roadless Acreage:	82,130 acres (includes 37,000 acres of Forest Service land)
Wilderness Status:	60,100 acres proposed for wilderness by BLM and Forest Service
Special Features:	Alpine tundra; cirque basins; lakes; scenic vistas
USGS Maps:	Cannibal Plateau, Mineral Mountain, Powderhorn Lakes, Rudolph Hill

The Cannibal and Calf Creek plateaus of the Powderhorn roadless area have been called the largest continuous expanse of alpine tundra in the lower 48 states. The plateaus create a seemingly endless, undulating plain of tundra, broken by several steep escarpments bejeweled by Powderhorn and other

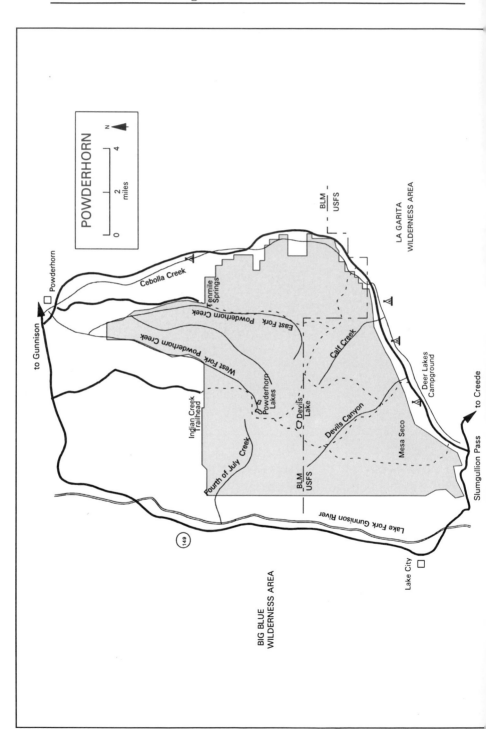

lakes. Few other areas in Colorado give rise to an equivalent sense of vastness, for the 12,000-foot elevation plateau affords unrestricted views of the San Juan, Elk and Sawatch ranges.

Cannibal Plateau was granted its name in recognition of the exploits of Alferd Packer, who in 1874 became Colorado's most notorious cannibal as he dined on his five companions while stranded at the western edge of the plateau. I hope your own hiking companions will consider more socially acceptable meals while visiting the area!

BLM shares administration of the alpine plateaus with the Forest Service. The BLM Powderhorn Primitive Area consists of the northern half of the two plateaus, and the Gunnison National Forest administers the southern reaches of the area. The agencies have combined to propose a single Powderhorn Wilderness Area.

BLM maintains the Indian Creek trail head for access into the area from the north. The trail head is approximately 10 miles up Indian Creek along a dirt road that departs from state Highway 149 about three miles west of the settlement of Powderhorn and the Cebolla Creek road intersection. Trails lead into the western half of the roadless area from this trail head, leading to Powderhorn Lakes, Hidden Lake and Devils Lake. From Powderhorn Lakes, an extension system of trails interconnects with Forest Service-administered trails to the south and creates several possibilities for loop trips.

Devils Lake can also be reached from the south, beginning at the Gunnison National Forest's Deer Lakes Campground along Forest Road 788. Head south from Lake City along Highway 149 and at Slumgullion Pass turn north to the campground. It is about an eight-mile hike from the campground to Devils Lake. Other trails onto Mesa Seco, Cannibal Plateau and Calf Creek Plateau branch off of the Devils Lake trail.

Trails into the eastern portion of the area begin at the end of the Ten Mile Springs road. This road heads south from Cebolla Creek just outside of Powderhorn and winds its way about eight miles to the roadless area boundary. Old vehicle trails lead south into the roadless area, one across Dempsey Parks to Powderhorn Park and the other along the East Fork of Powderhorn Creek.

John Fielder

7 REDCLOUD PEAK

Location:	Five miles southwest of Lake City
Elevation Range:	9,000 – 14,034 feet
Vegetation/Ecosystem:	Spruce-fir; aspen; willows; alpine tundra
Roadless Acreage:	41,000 acres
Wilderness Status:	29,500 acres proposed for wilderness by BLM*
Special Features:	Two 14,000-foot peaks; Cooper Lake; glacial valleys
USGS Maps:	Lake City, Lake San Cristobal, Redcloud Peak, Uncompahgre Peak

*BLM's favorable wilderness recommendation for Handies Peak was vetoed by Interior Secretary Manuel Lujan in September 1991.

The Redcloud Peak roadless area contains some of the most spectacular alpine country in Colorado — indeed, in the United States. Within it are two of

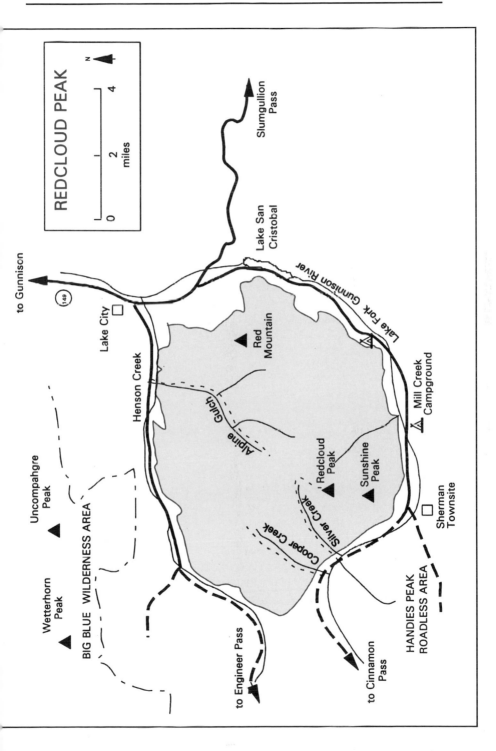

REDCLOUD PEAK

N

0   2   4
miles

to Gunnison

(149)

Lake City

Henson Creek

Uncompahgre Peak

Wetterhorn Peak

BIG BLUE WILDERNESS AREA

Slumgullion Pass

Lake San Cristobal

Lake Fork Gunnison River

Red Mountain

Alpine Gulch

Mill Creek Campground

Redcloud Peak

Sunshine Peak

Silver Creek

Cooper Creek

Sherman Townsite

HANDIES PEAK ROADLESS AREA

to Engineer Pass

to Cinnamon Pass

Colorado's 14,000-foot peaks: 14,034-foot Redcloud Peak and 14,001-foot Sunshine Peak. The mountains plunge from 14,000 feet to the 9,000-foot Lake Fork valley in a horizontal distance of less than a mile. The steep lower valleys are of glacial origin, blanketed by spruce-fir forests and stands of aspen.

Three main drainages dissect the area. Of these, Alpine Gulch is the largest, its tributaries collecting runoff from the northeastern slopes of the area. Silver Creek and Cooper Creek drain the western flanks of the high peaks, and Cooper Lake is nestled high at the head of Cooper Creek. Trails traverse each of these drainages, providing recreational access to the high peaks and alpine tundra. The prospect of bagging the fourteeners draws many hikers to the area.

Silver Creek is the most popular trail because it is the most direct route to the two fourteeners. Silver Creek is a tributary of the Lake Fork of the Gunnison. From Lake City, head south out of town, past Lake San Cristobal and the BLM's Mill Creek Campground, and continue right on the Cinnamon Pass road at the abandoned townsite of Sherman. The Silver Creek trail head is three miles on the right. The trail climbs gradually above timberline through a broad alpine valley to the saddle northeast of Redcloud Peak. From there, it is a short climb up the ridge to the summit. Total distance from the trailhead is about five miles. Sunshine Peak is 1.5 miles south along the summit ridge from Redcloud. Either backtrack to return to the trail head or descend steeply into the gulch on the west side of the saddle between the peaks and join up with Silver Creek midway along its length.

Cooper Creek begins one mile past Silver Creek on the Cinnamon Pass road. The valley of Cooper Creek is similar to that of Silver Creek, but a small alpine lake graces the head of this valley. The Cooper Creek trail provides access to several unnamed 13,000-foot peaks.

Alpine Gulch is the longest valley in the area and offers a scenic northern approach for climbs of Redcloud Peak. Climb out of cirque basins of either of the western branches to reach the saddle on the north side of Redcloud Peak, approximately eight miles from the trail head. To reach Alpine Gulch, take the Henson Creek road west from Lake City. Alpine Gulch intersects Henson Creek just over two miles up the creek. The Alpine Gulch trail is less frequently used than other trails because of the difficult crossing of Henson Creek that is required. In spring and early summer, snowmelt makes crossing Henson Creek a hazardous undertaking. For that reason, late summer and fall are recommended seasons for Alpine Gulch. The trail leads to several old mines and prospects and provides access to the backside of Red Mountain.

A deposit of alunite underlies Red Mountain, which forms the scenic backdrop to Lake City. Alunite is an alternate ore to bauxite for producing aluminum, with biproducts of sulfuric acid and potash. A mining company approached the BLM in 1983 to lease and mine this deposit. BLM prepared an environmental assessment of a proposed open-pit mine, which indicated that 2,000 feet would be removed from the top of Red Mountain and that the upper end of Alpine Gulch would be turned into a huge tailings pile of tockpiled ore. Congress later banned the issuance of mineral leases within wilderness study areas, so no final decision was ever reached by BLM on the lease application, though all indications were that it would be denied.

8 SQUAW and PAPOOSE CANYONS

Location:	40 miles northwest of Cortez
Elevation Range:	5,100 – 6,600 feet
Vegetation/Ecosystem:	Cottonwoods; sagebrush; piñon-juniper
Roadless Acreage:	14,180 acres
Wilderness Status:	Not proposed for wilderness by BLM
Special Features:	Archaeological resources; rare and diverse reptiles and amphibians
USGS Maps:	Champagne Spring, Monument Canyon (15'), Ruin Canyon

Squaw and Papoose canyons generally parallel each other, trending northeast to southwest as they cross the Colorado-Utah border. The canyons begin as rocky arroyos but rapidly cut into the Dakota Sandstone and the Morrison Formation to form rugged, steep canyon walls of exposed rock outcrops, boulders and talus slopes.

Both canyons are rich in archaeological resources. This region of Colorado and Utah contains one of the greatest concentrations of Anasazi sites, as many as 40 to 60 sites per square mile, and includes round towers, Hovenweep towers, pit houses, pueblos, cliff dwellings, lithic scatter, pottery shards, agricultural sites and a wide variety of pictographs and petroglyphs. Please don't deface or remove these traces of ancient cultures; leave them for others to observe and enjoy.

Squaw and Papoose canyons support numerous species of wildlife, many of which have been displaced from the surrounding uplands as a result of agricultural and other development activities. Larger mammalian species include deer, mountain lion and black bear. The diverse topography allows for a similar abundance of bird species, including resident golden eagles and migratory bald eagles. Peregrine falcons may occasionally visit the area. Squaw and Papoose canyons are considered to have the most abundant and diverse reptile and amphibian population in Colorado, including many rare and localized species and subspecies.

A wide variety of vegetation occurs in the area, beginning with the piñon-juniper forest and sagebrush that dominate the canyon rims. The slopes contain trees and shrubs including rabbitbrush, Mormon-tea, mountain-mahogany, Gambel oak, serviceberry and cliffrose, among others. Vegetation is thicker along the canyon floors. There you will find numerous grasses; cactus and yucca; wildflowers such as Indian paintbrush, penstemon, yarrow, phlox and lupine; and riparian flora including rushes, sedges, cattails, willows, tamarisk, boxelder, and cottonwoods.

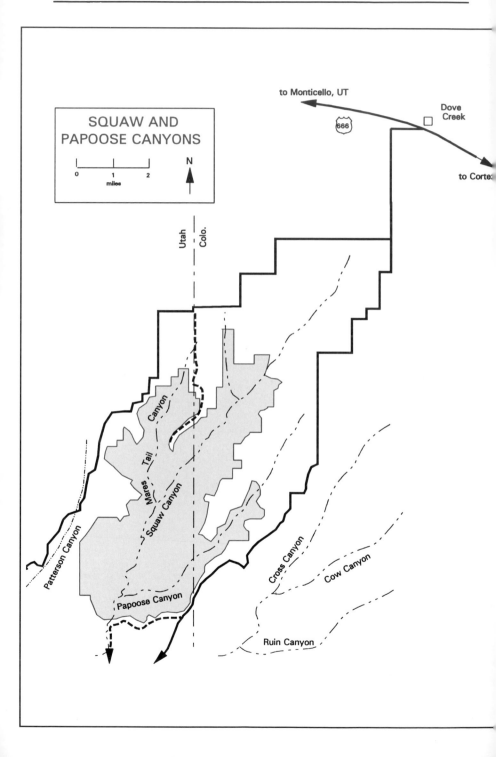

SQUAW AND
PAPOOSE CANYONS

0   1   2
miles

N

to Monticello, UT

Dove
Creek

666

to Cortez

Utah

Colo.

Patterson Canyon

Mares Tail Canyon

Squaw Canyon

Papoose Canyon

Cross Canyon

Cow Canyon

Ruin Canyon

Sunrise on sandstone walls and Utah's Abajo Mountains,
Squaw/Papoose Canyon Wilderness Study Area. John Fielder photograph.

The perennial streams that run in both canyons consist largely of runoff from agricultural fields. Be cautious about drinking the water, even if treated.

To reach the west side of Squaw Canyon, head west from Dove Creek and then zigzag on farm roads southwest toward the state line. Follow a road south along the state line that dead-ends on the rim of the canyon in about four miles. From this point, you can scramble several hundred feet into the canyon bottom and hike four miles upstream to private land or head downstream about eight miles to the confluence of Papoose Canyon. The branching nature of the two canyons creates the opportunity for extended, multiday explorations of the canyons and their many fascinating cultural treasures. Papoose Canyon is around nine miles in length. From its head, strike out due west until you reach the rim of Squaw Canyon, at which point you will be nearly opposite your starting point on the west rim.

There is also road access to lower Squaw Canyon, below its confluence with Papoose. Take the road west from Dove Creek but rather than heading southwest for the state line, drive straight south to the east side of Squaw Canyon. Follow the road southwest along the mesa between Papoose Canyon and Cross Canyon. The road deteriorates from this point and ultimately may be impassable beyond the state line to the bottom of Squaw Canyon. The rim here offers sweeping views of the canyon system. Depending upon where you leave your vehicle, drop into the canyon bottom and head upstream a mile or so to the confluence of Squaw and Papoose canyons. You can hike up and back in either of the canyons or make a loop through both.

TABEGUACHE

Location:	Six miles north of Nucla
Elevation Range:	5,600 – 7,400 feet
Vegetation/Ecosystem:	Cottonwood riparian; piñon-juniper; ponderosa pine; oakbrush
Roadless Acreage:	19,040 acres (includes 10,240 acres of Forest Service land)
Wilderness Status:	7,743 acres proposed for wilderness by BLM
Special Features:	Perennial stream; slickrock canyon; ponderosa forest
USGS Maps:	Nucla, Windy Point

The Tabeguache roadless area includes 14 miles of Tabeguache Creek and eight miles of the North Fork of Tabeguache Creek, though only six miles of the creek are on BLM land. Both creeks begin in fertile subalpine bowls atop the Uncompahgre Plateau in the National Forest and shortly plunge into extraordinarily steep walled, lush canyons. Mighty old-growth aspen forests, many trees with diameters in excess of three feet, are scattered across slopes throughout the watershed of the North Fork.

The hikes described here are confined to the lower segment of the canyon that traverses BLM land. At the downstream end of Tabeguache Canyon are found sparse piñon-juniper woodland, sagebrush flats and lowland riparian vegetation. Moving upward, vegetation changes to Gambel oak and other types of brushland, ponderosa pine–Douglas-fir forest, aspen and spruce-fir interspersed with upland meadows. This transition is far from orderly, however. Instead, the various biomes interfinger with one another in a manner that offers many strange combinations of scenery and habitat. This is caused primarily by cool mountain air flowing down the canyon of Tabeguache Creek, carrying biological characteristics of the uplands with it. As a result, hikers entering the area from the Pinto Mesa area, for example, find themselves passing downward from the upper Sonoran life zone, dominated by piñon and juniper, into the ponderosa–Douglas-fir of the transition zone along the stream; this zone is normally found at higher elevations.

A trail from Pinto Mesa takes you directly into the heart of the ponderosa–Douglas-fir transition zone. Take Forest Road 503 toward Columbine Pass north from Nucla. Approximately eight miles from town, Forest Road 660 turns west and climbs onto Pinto Mesa. Skirt an agricultural field, turn north and park another mile farther on where the road becomes severely eroded. This eroded four-wheel-drive trail turns into a foot and horse trail identified

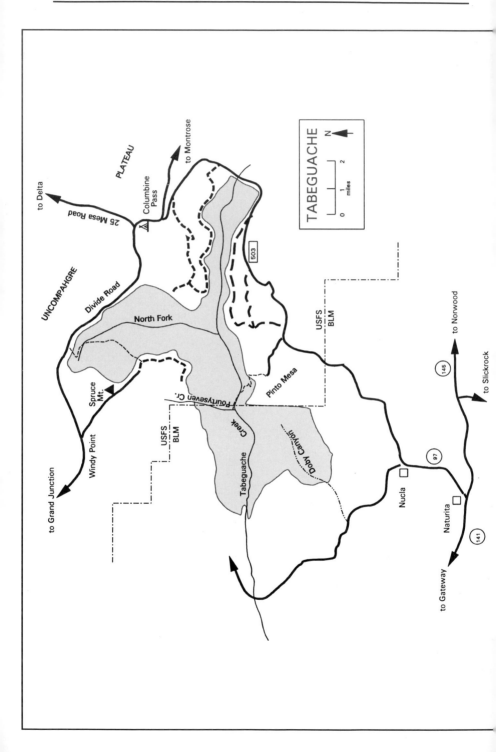

Tabeguache Creek, Tabeguache Creek Wilderness Study Area. Eric Finstick photograph.

by a sign as the Indian Trail. The trail switchbacks into the canyon bottom through dense oakbrush and ultimately disappears in thick brush along the stream bank. The canyon walls are relatively close together at this point and are composed of Wingate Sandstone cliffs overlain by Entrada Sandstone with a thin or nonexistent layer of intervening Kayenta caprock. The stately ponderosas that line the creek bottom are set in brilliant contrast against these red canyon walls. Tabeguache Creek is a raging torrent in early spring, but a large ponderosa that has fallen across the creek several hundred yards downstream from the trail creates a natural bridge if the creek cannot be forded. A faint trail parallels the creek downstream to Forty-seven Creek.

The mouth of Tabeguache Canyon is also accessible from Nucla. Head northwest out of town, past old coal mines, six or seven miles to a road that forks to the right. This path takes you to the boundary of the roadless area, from which you can hike cross-country to the canyon rim. The canyon walls are low and easily descended, though thick riparian growth along the streambank makes travel difficult. It is easier to parallel the creek through the piñon-juniper forests a few hundred feet above the creek. The streambed itself provides the easiest hiking route during late summer and autumn low water, though boulder hopping and numerous stream crossings are required.

John Fielder

10 WEBER MOUNTAIN and MENEFEE MOUNTAIN

Location:	20 miles east of Cortez
Elevation Range:	6,500 – 8,300 feet
Vegetation/Ecosystem:	Piñon-juniper; oakbrush; mountain-mahogany; ponderosa pine; Douglas-fir
Roadless Acreage:	13,500 acres
Wilderness Status:	Not proposed for wilderness by BLM
Special Features:	Scenic buttes; bighorn sheep; spotted owl
USGS Maps:	Mancos, Thompson Park, Trail Canyon

Weber and Menefee mountains are wilderness islands amid the developed agricultural lands of the Mancos River Valley. As such, they provide extremely important undisturbed wildlife habitat. Both mountains are prominent buttes, rising from 6,500 to 8,300 feet, capped with resistant Point Lookout Sandstone that creates a girdling barrier of cliffs. These sheer cliffs, combined with dense vegetation, create the almost impenetrable solitude that many species of wildlife

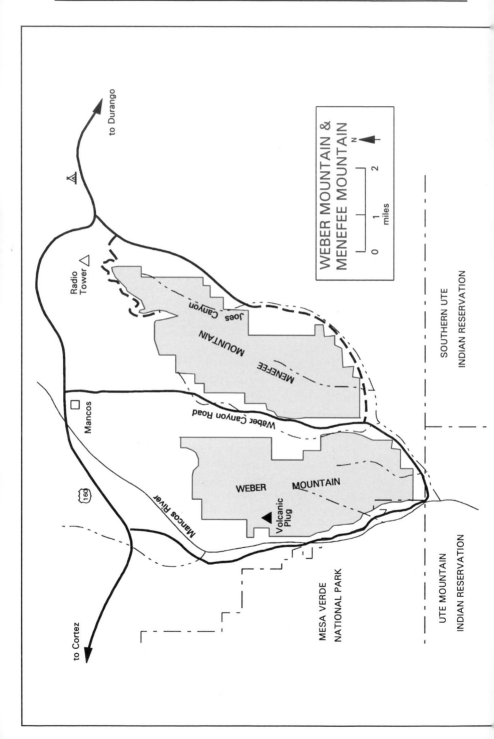

WEBER MOUNTAIN &
MENEFEE MOUNTAIN

0   1   2
miles

N

to Durango

Radio
Tower

Joes Canyon

MENEFEE MOUNTAIN

Weber Canyon Road

Mancos

Mancos River

160

to Cortez

WEBER   MOUNTAIN

Volcanic
Plug

MESA VERDE
NATIONAL PARK

UTE MOUNTAIN
INDIAN RESERVATION

SOUTHERN UTE
INDIAN RESERVATION

find so necessary. Around the mountains, farming and ranching have stripped the land, leaving good vegetative cover only on the mountains.

Mule deer herds migrate along the bottom slopes of the mountains for winter range. Weber Mountain and adjacent Menefee Mountain provide a valuable refuge, offering ridge tops that blow free of snow and protective valleys between. Deer can migrate through the area without any manmade obstructions, to the lower, warmer lands of the Ute Mountain Indian Reservation to the south. A small herd of bighorn sheep, originally introduced into adjacent Mesa Verde National Park in 1946, frequents Weber Mountain. Perhaps 20 black bears, up to 10 mountain lions and a number of bobcats inhabit the area as well. Golden eagle nests have been identified on Menefee Mountain. The endangered Mexican spotted owl has been sighted on the Ute Reservation immediately south and in adjacent Mesa Verde National Park.

Vegetation consists of piñon-juniper forest, oakbrush and mountain-mahogany with scattered stands of Douglas-fir and ponderosa pine above 7,000 feet. The ruggedness creates prime opportunities for hiking, backpacking and climbing, and the cliff tops offer dramatic vantage points for sightseeing and photography.

Weber and Menefee mountains offer wonderful opportunities for solitude, fine scenery and backcountry recreation in close proximity to Mesa Verde National Park. The existing Mesa Verde Wilderness is closed to recreational use, as is all of the backcountry in Mesa Verde, for the purpose of protecting the archaeological sites in the National Park.

Weber Mountain, the western of the two mountains, is prominent in the view from the main entrance road into the park. Two large canyons drain the south end of the mountain and offer rugged routes to the mountain crest. The Mancos River Valley road, accessible from Highway 160 west of Mancos, parallels the western edge of the mountain, and the Weber Canyon road that heads south from the town of Mancos parallels the eastern edge. The spires and pinnacles of an intrusive volcanic plug midway down the west side of the mountain offer an interesting destination for short hikes. However, most hikes in Weber Mountain require bushwhacking through dense brush.

The west side of Menefee Mountain is generally barricaded by private land from the Weber Canyon road. Better hiking opportunities are found on the east side near Joes Canyon. Take Highway 160 east from Mancos and turn south on a dirt road at the large horseshoe curve atop the hill. One branch of this road ascends the mountain to several radio towers, from which point you can hike south along the top of the mountain. Another branch of the road heads south, where in about five miles a four-wheel-drive trail backtracks north up Joes Canyon near an old cabin. Joes Canyon is covered with ponderosa pines and Douglas-fir and provides a pleasant hike in a secluded setting.

MIDWEST
COLORADO

Opposite: Black Rocks and the Colorado River, Ruby Canyon, Black Ridge Canyons Wilderness Study Area. John Fielder photograph.

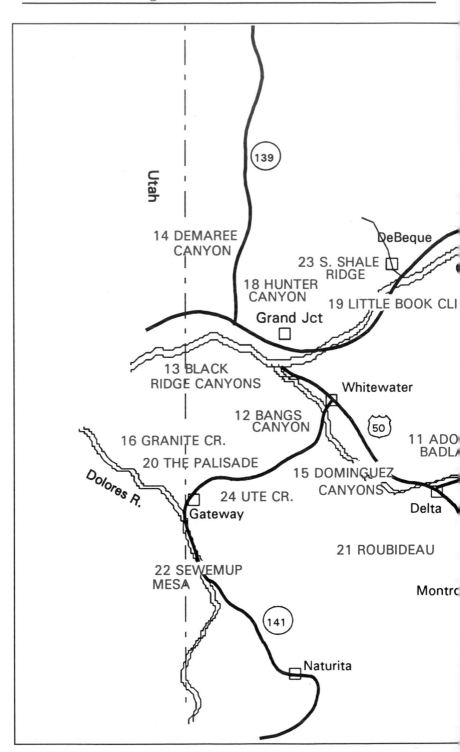

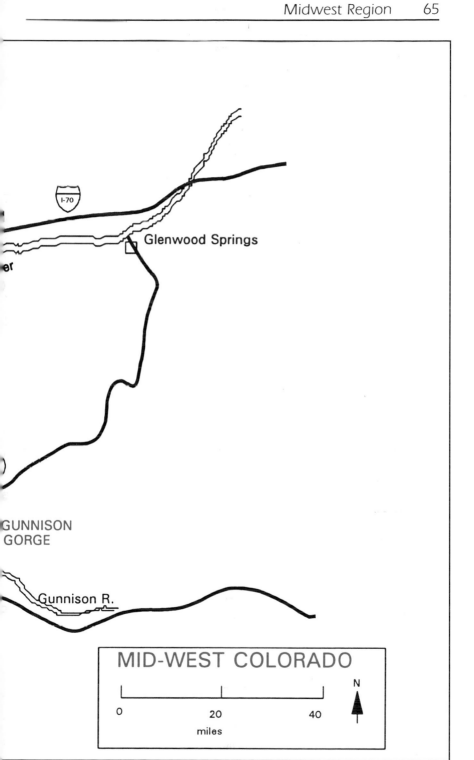

I-70

Glenwood Springs

GUNNISON
GORGE

Gunnison R.

MID-WEST COLORADO

0   20   40
miles

N

Mark Pearson

11   ADOBE BADLANDS

Location:	Three miles north of Delta
Elevation Range:	5,200 – 8,300 feet
Vegetation/Ecosystem:	Sagebrush; piñon-juniper
Roadless Acreage:	10,560 acres
Wilderness Status:	Not proposed for wilderness by BLM
Special Features:	Scenic vistas; badlands topography
USGS Maps:	North Delta, Point Creek

Adobe Badlands roadless area is notable for its mazelike adobe formations of gray and yellow Mancos Shale interspersed with intriguing canyons, mesas and arroyos on the southern slopes of the Grand Mesa. The badlands offer scenic vistas of Grand Mesa, the Uncompahgre Plateau, and the San Juan Mountains. Two endangered cactus species, the spineless hedgehog cactus and *Sclerocactus glaucidus*, are thought to inhabit the area.

At first glimpse, the Adobe Badlands appear unforgiving and void of life, but with closer inspection, wildlife is seen to flourish everywhere. Birds such as the house finch, Gambel's quail and piñon jay are common in the area,

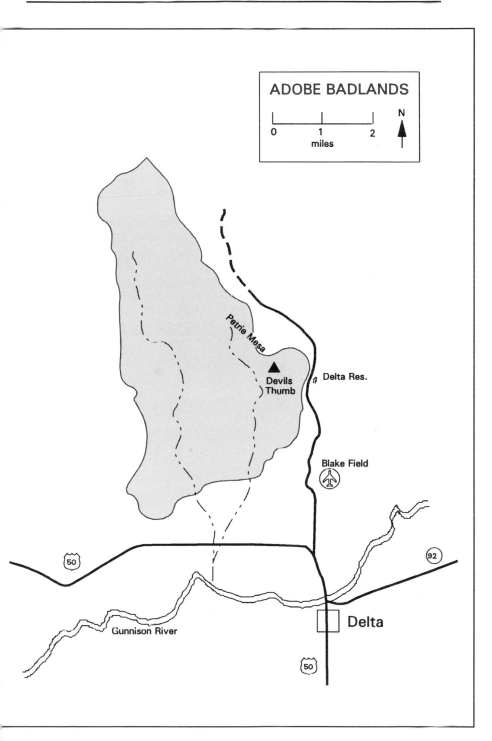

and the turkey vulture, red-tailed hawk and golden eagle are occasionally seen. Desert striped whipsnakes and northern sagebrush lizards are some of the common reptiles found in the Adobes. Pronghorn are also found roaming the slopes of the area.

The Mancos Shale that comprises the badlands was deposited between 135 million to 65 million years ago by an ancient sea. Marine fossils from that period can be found in the shale. Volcanic eruptions later deposited a basaltic caprock that now forms the top of Grand Mesa. Erosion has since created the spectacular badlands that now occupy much of the area.

The roadless area lies immediately north of Highway 50 outside of Delta. Take the airport road north at the highway curve in north Delta and veer west just below the hilltop runway. This road skirts past an abandoned reservoir and angles toward the Grand Mesa along the eastern side of Adobe Badlands. Devils Thumb, a prominent eroded pinnacle, juts from the end of Petrie Mesa and is a short hike from the road. Park near the abandoned reservoir, approximately 2.5 miles north of the airport, and head cross-country to the thumb. An alternative is to continue on the road to the north side of Petrie Mesa and hike the obvious abandoned four-wheel-drive trail up the mesa and out its length to Devils Thumb. There are many vantage points for stunning views of the San Juan Mountains, particularly when the peaks are snow covered in spring or fall.

Mark Pearson

12   BANGS CANYON

Location:	Five miles south of Grand Junction
Elevation Range:	4,900 – 8,000 feet
Vegetation/Ecosystem:	Piñon-juniper; sagebrush; Douglas-fir; aspen
Roadless Acreage:	21,130 acres
Wilderness Status:	Not proposed for wilderness by BLM
Special Features:	Ecological transition; perennial streams
USGS Maps:	Island Mesa, Whitewater

Bangs Canyon provides remarkable backcountry recreation opportunities just minutes from downtown Grand Junction. Located southeast of the Colorado National Monument, the area takes in several wild canyons, including Bangs Canyon and North East Creek. Water has cut through the Morrison and Entrada sediments to form these hideaways on the flanks of the Uncompahgre Uplift. Vegetation ranges from Douglas-fir and aspen on the Uncompahgre Plateau to saltbush desert on the south bank of the Gunnison River.

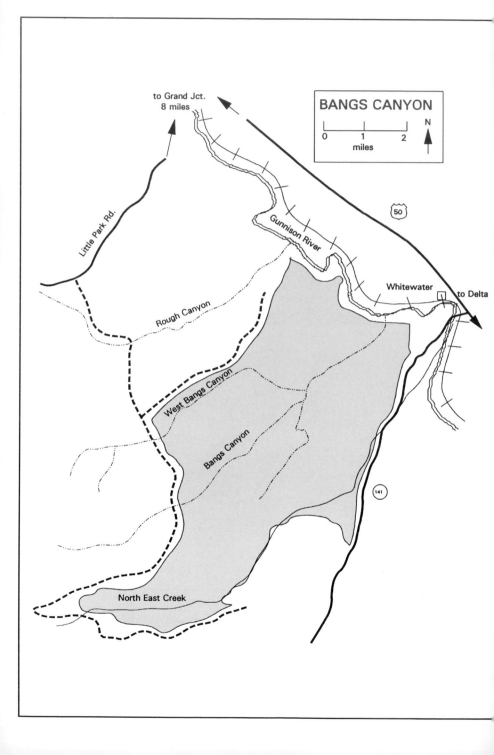

Though near to Grand Junction, Bangs Canyon possesses a great sense of remoteness and solitude. The boundaries of the area are largely defined by rough four-wheel-drive roads and by the Gunnison River. Access to the western edge of the area from Grand Junction is relatively quick, but it may take a couple of hours to get to the upper reaches of North East Creek on the south end of the area. North East Creek carves a scenic canyon, lined with cottonwoods and pools, along state Highway 141 on the eastern side of the unit.

Access to Bangs Canyon is gained via Little Park Road south of Grand Junction. From downtown Grand Junction, follow the signs to the Colorado National Monument. Take Broadway across the Colorado River, turn left onto Monument Road, and turn left almost immediately onto Rosevale Road. Rosevale Road curves around a corner and in several blocks intersects Little Park Road. Follow Little Park south approximately six miles (1.5 miles beyond the end of the pavement) to a dirt road that branches south. This road goes directly to Bangs Canyon and forms the western boundary of the roadless area.

The first drainage crossed is Rough Canyon. Though not part of the Bangs Canyon roadless area, Rough Canyon is a pleasant hike that includes pools, waterfalls and petroglyphs. A short two-mile hike upstream will return you close to the Little Park Road.

West Bangs Canyon is three miles beyond Rough Canyon, and Bangs Canyon is another two miles farther. You can follow either branch of the canyon three or four miles downstream to the confluence with the other branch; from there it is another three miles to the Gunnison River. These canyons are cut largely through the Morrison Formation, which creates soft canyon walls of green and gray shale. The canyons are relatively broad and shallow. Several miles more travel southwest brings you to North East Creek, a rugged canyon with a perennial stream. Highway 141 is approximately eight miles down North East Creek.

John Fielder

13   BLACK RIDGE CANYONS

Location:	10 miles west of Grand Junction
Elevation Range:	4,700 – 6,800 feet
Vegetation/Ecosystem:	Piñon-juniper; sagebrush; cottonwoods
Roadless Acreage:	75,000 acres
Wilderness Status:	73,937 acres proposed for wilderness by BLM
Special Features:	Colorado River; arches; slickrock canyons; endangered species; desert bighorn sheep
USGS Maps:	Battleship Rock, Bitter Creek Well, Colorado National Monument, Mack, Ruby Canyon, Sieber Canyon, Westwater 4 SE

Black Ridge is an outstanding example of deep, sheer-walled slickrock canyons. The scenery is somewhat similar to that of Colorado National Monument but

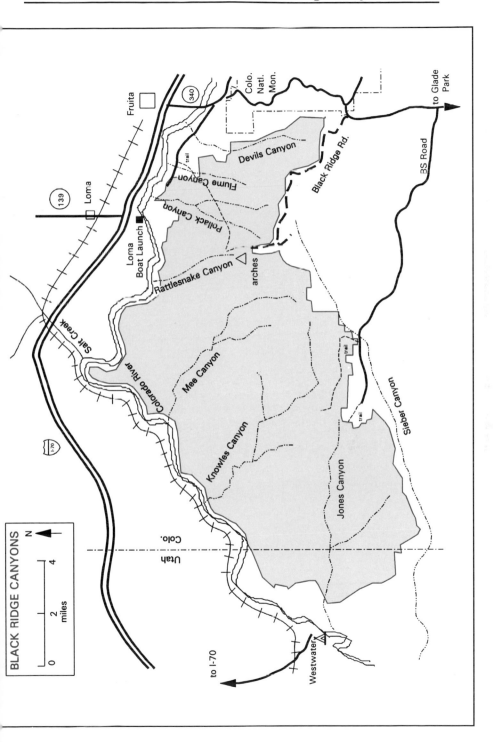

BLACK RIDGE CANYONS

N

0   2   4
miles

Fruita

340

Colo. Natl. Mon.

to Glade Park

BS Road

Black Ridge Rd.

139

Loma

Devils Canyon

Flume Canyon

trail

Pollack Canyon

Loma Boat Launch

Rattlesnake Canyon

arches

trail

Salt Creek

Colorado River

Mee Canyon

trail

Sieber Canyon

I-70

Knowles Canyon

Jones Canyon

Utah   Colo.

to I-70

Westwater

is much more varied. Whereas the Monument features only relatively short, dry canyons and a few rock pinnacles, Black Ridge contains three major canyon systems much longer than anything in the Monument, innumerable spires and pinnacles, the second greatest concentration of natural arches in the Southwest, perennial streams with rich riparian vegetation, a huge 300-foot cavern cut by a stream meander in Mee Canyon and about 20 miles of frontage along the Colorado River in Ruby and Horsethief canyons. This stretch of the Colorado River has been recommended for Scenic designation under the Wild and Scenic Rivers Act. BLM estimates that the river alone receives 7,000 visitor days of use per year.

Black Ridge contains critical wildlife habitat for many species. Desert bighorn sheep have been reintroduced into the area; the herd presently consists of 30 to 40 animals. Deer, mountain lion and many raptors also inhabit Black Ridge. The river corridor provides wintering grounds for bald eagles, and active golden eagle nesting sites exist within the area.

Black Ridge is also home to several rare and endangered species. These include four species of endangered fish in the Colorado River (the humpback chub, Colorado River squawfish, bonytail chub and razorback sucker) as well as a rare butterfly, *Papilio indra minori*.

Black Ridge is a large area with many and varied access points. The Colorado River is one of the most popular avenues for visiting Black Ridge, and the segment from Loma to the Westwater ranger station is flat water suitable for most types of watercraft. To find the Loma boat launch, take the Loma exit on Interstate 70 (I-70) west of Grand Junction, drive south across the overpass and follow the signs left to the boat ramp. The hidden mouth of Rattlesnake Canyon is 3.3 miles downstream on river left. A steep climb up Rattlesnake Canyon will take you to the arches in the Entrada Sandstone along the canyon rim, but the overland access route to the arches described below is less strenuous. Mee Canyon, 14 miles downstream from Loma, is a popular campsite and river hike. Pinnacles, windows and turrets line the canyon mouth and occur in groups throughout the lower several miles of the canyon. Other popular campsites along the river include those at Black Rocks, two miles beyond Mee Canyon, and at the mouth of Knowles Canyon, several miles farther downstream. Knowles Canyon offers many miles of hiking and tributaries. The Westwater ranger station, and the takeout for this segment of the river, is 25 river miles from Loma. Rafting beyond the ranger station and through Westwater Canyon requires a permit from BLM. The Westwater Ranger Station is at the end of an eight-mile gravel road which leads to I-70 at the Westwater Exit, just over the Utah state line.

The Rattlesnake Canyon arches have gained increasing attention in recent years. In recognition of this, BLM has constructed a trail to the arches from the river near Fruita and has also placed primitive facilities at the end of the four-wheel-drive road to the arches. This hiking trail, surprisingly steep in places, begins west of Fruita in the mouth of Flume Canyon and traverses approximately four miles across East and West Pollock canyons to Rattlesnake Canyon. The trail is reached via Highway 340 south from Fruita. Turn right at the Kingswood Estates subdivision and follow the road a couple of miles west to the trailhead in Flume Canyon.

The arches can also be reached via a rough, eight-mile four-wheel-drive road that begins just outside the Colorado National Monument. Take the rim drive in the Monument, turn south onto the dirt road to Glade Park midway along the rim drive and turn west onto the Black Ridge Hunter Access Road. This road heads to a couple of radio transmitters and then follows the north slope of Black Ridge to Rattlesnake Canyon. BLM has constructed a parking area at the end of the road, and a short trail takes you to the arches, of which there are a dozen scattered along a mile of the canyon rim. Be warned, however, that this road is entirely impassable when wet owing to the Morrison Shale on which it is built.

BLM has constructed two trail heads in the Twenty-eight Hole country for access to the more remote corners of Black Ridge. These trail heads are reached by traveling through the Monument to the Glade Park store, then heading a mile north to the first major road west. Follow this road (BS Road) 12 miles west to the Knowles Canyon trail head, just after you cross Twenty-eight Hole wash (or Sieber Canyon). A 1.5-mile trail leads to a four-wheel-drive trail that skirts the head of Knowles Canyon. This trail can be followed into the canyon, or you can pioneer your own route into the bottom.

The second trail head is several miles farther west. A locked gate denotes the end of the public road and also marks the trailhead to Jones Canyon. This trail head is one of your best bets for seeing few other people.

Sandstone arch, Rattlesnake Canyon, Black Ridge Canyons Wilderness Study Area. John Fielder photograph.

Mark Pearson

14   DEMAREE CANYON

Location:	25 miles northwest of Grand Junction
Elevation Range:	5,000 –7,500 feet
Vegetation/Ecosystem:	Douglas-fir; piñon-juniper; oakbrush-mountain-mahogany; greasewood; sagebrush
Roadless Acreage:	21,050 acres
Wilderness Status:	Not proposed for wilderness by BLM
Special Features:	Desert scenery; views of the La Sal Mountains
USGS Maps:	Carbonera, Howard Canyon

Demaree Canyon is a chunk of the wild canyons of the Book Cliffs in extreme western Colorado. The roadless area consists of the Book Cliff escarpment, rising more than 2,500 feet out of the featureless desert plains of the Grand Valley and culminating in rugged ridges. Four large canyons dissect this desolate terrain, spanning the cliff front between East and West Salt creeks.

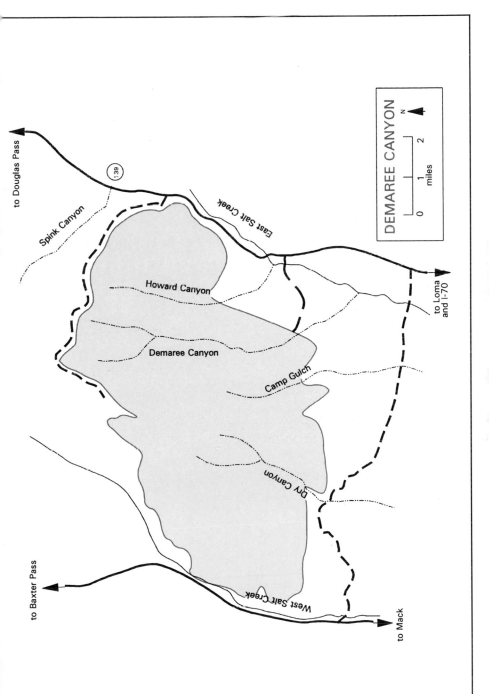

to Douglas Pass

Spink Canyon

139

East Salt Creek

Howard Canyon

Demaree Canyon

Camp Gulch

Dry Canyon

to Loma and I-70

to Baxter Pass

West Salt Creek

to Mack

DEMAREE CANYON

N

0   1   2
miles

The canyons of Demaree are cut through the tan and brown sandstones of the Mesa Verde Group, underlain by gray Mancos Shale. Forests of piñon and juniper blanket the steep slopes of uplifted cliffs, interspersed with dense thickets of mountain-mahogany and oakbrush. Intermittent streams occasionally carve bowls and channels through the soft sandstone.

Hikers gain an immediate sense of intimacy upon entering a canyon from the open plain of the Grand Valley. Splashes of cactus wildflowers enliven the otherwise gray and forest-green backdrop. The canyons gradually close in and lead to steep head walls. An oil and gas exploration road bladed across the tops of these imposing slopes forms the northern boundary of the roadless area. Stirring views of the snow-capped La Sal Mountains, rising from behind the red-rock canyons of the Uncompahgre Plateau, are gained from these ridges.

Demaree Canyon is readily accessible from either east or west. The eastern boundary of the unit is the Douglas Pass road, Highway 139. Take the highway north from I-70 at the Loma exit to a point about 1.5 miles north of the Mesa-Garfield county line. A road takes off to the west, skirts a stock pond and immediately crosses East Salt Creek, which is a shallow ford during all but the height of spring runoff. The road will take you to the mouth of Demaree Canyon a mile farther on, at which point you can abandon your vehicle for hiking boots. The streambed of Demaree Canyon makes a pleasant hiking path and leads past outcrops of sandstone and several narrow channels to the source of the canyon.

Several miles farther along Highway 139, an oil and gas exploration road climbs steeply out of East Salt Creek and gains the ridge top. This road forms the northern boundary of Demaree Canyon. Hikers can drop into Howard and Demaree canyons, Camp Gulch, or Dry Canyon from this road, but remember the steep incline will be awaiting your return to your vehicle.

Access to Demaree Canyon from the west is via the Baxter Pass road. From Loma, head west on old Highway 50 to Mack and follow the signs to Baxter Pass and Bonanza, Utah. The Mitchell Road turns east from this road one mile north of the Mesa-Garfield county line. The Mitchell Road generally forms the southern boundary of the Demaree Canyon roadless area and takes you directly to the mouth of Dry Canyon. An oil and gas road has been punched a couple of miles up this canyon, but the canyon is pristine beyond the end of the road.

JohnFielder

15 DOMINGUEZ CANYONS

Location:	20 miles southeast of Grand Junction
Elevation Range:	4,800 – 9,000 feet
Vegetation/Ecosystem:	Cottonwood riparian zone; piñon-juniper; ponderosa and Douglas-fir; aspen and spruce
Roadless Acreage:	90,050 acres (includes 11,000 acres of Forest Service land)
Wilderness Status:	73,568 acres proposed for wilderness by BLM
Special Features:	Waterfalls and pools; petroglyphs; desert bighorn sheep
USGS Maps:	Dominguez, Escalante Forks, Good Point, Jacks Canyon, Keith Creek, Triangle Mesa

Big and Little Dominguez canyons make up a spectacular slickrock canyon wilderness. The canyons are endowed with the components of a desert paradise

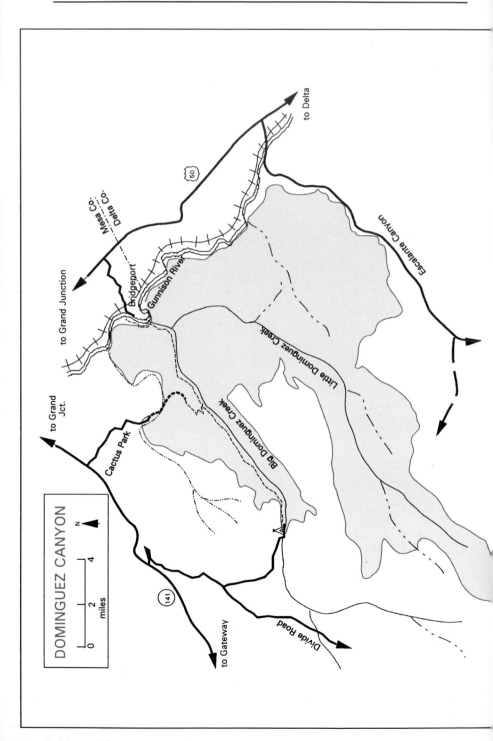

DOMINGUEZ CANYON

N

0   2   4
miles

to Grand Jct.

Cactus Park

to Gateway

141

Divide Road

Big Dominguez Creek

Little Dominguez Creek

Escalante Canyon

Gunnison River

Bridgeport

Mesa Co.
Delta Co.

50

to Grand Junction

to Delta

— perennial streams and plunge pools carved out of glistening black schist, brilliant red sandstone walls, gracious cottonwoods, desert bighorn sheep, an endangered cactus (the spineless hedgehog), numerous petroglyph panels and many soaring raptors.

The canyons drain the northeastern corner of the Uncompahgre Plateau and front the Gunnison River for almost 15 miles. Little Dominguez is the longer of the two, approximately 20 miles from top to bottom. It joins larger Big Dominguez canyon just before their confluence with the Gunnison River. The area is the largest BLM roadless area in the state and spans an extraordinary array of ecosystems, ranging from upper Sonoran piñon-juniper desert along the Gunnison through Douglas-fir and ponderosa pine to aspen and spruce-fir forests in the highest reaches.

Big Dominguez Canyon is the more accessible of the two. The upper and middle sections are reached via Highway 141 southwest of Whitewater. BLM has constructed a primitive trail from the Cactus Park area into the middle of Big Dominguez. The Cactus Park turnoff is clearly marked on the highway approximately nine miles from Whitewater. An initially good dirt road takes you seven miles to the rim of the canyon (the last couple of miles require a high-clearance vehicle), where a short, steep and primitive marked trail drops to the canyon floor. It is several miles downstream from this point to the confluence with Little Dominguez. A mile or so above the confluence are a 30-foot slot waterfall and several large boulders covered with petroglyphs.

BLM's Dominguez Campground provides the jumping-off point for hikes from the head of the canyon. The campground is reached via Highway 141 also, but the turnoff is the Divide Road, five miles beyond the Cactus Park road. The Divide Road is a well-maintained Forest Service road that accesses the Uncompahgre Plateau. After climbing onto the plateau, a sign identifies the turnoff to Dominguez Campground, another four or five miles beyond the Divide Road. The campground is a pleasant, shaded spot along Big Dominguez Creek at the head of the roadless area. From here, it is perhaps 10 or 12 miles down the canyon to the confluence with Little Dominguez and about eight miles to the Cactus Park trail.

Another popular access to Dominguez is the mouth of the canyon via the Gunnison River. The Gunnison River through the Dominguez Canyon section is an easy raft or canoe trip, and the canyon mouth is a favored campsite. Waterfalls and pools mark the entrance of the canyon, and the confluence of Big and Little Dominguez is only a mile up the canyon. Boaters generally launch at the Escalante Canyon bridge several miles downstream from Delta (accessed from Highway 50) and can take out at Bridgeport or the Highway 141 bridge at the town of Whitewater.

In previous years, the public was able to reach Dominguez across a decrepit wooden bridge at Bridgeport, just a few hundred yards downstream of the canyon mouth. The bridge is private; it has been condemned by BLM and is now off limits to public use. It is still possible to cross the river at this point in a canoe or other watercraft, but please respect the closure of the bridge. Bridgeport is reached via a dirt road that leaves Highway 50 about a mile east of the Mesa-Delta county line.

Dominguez is a large and varied area that can easily absorb several days or a week of exploration. Intrepid hikers can make an adventurous multiday backpack out of a circuit of both Big and Little Dominguez canyons. Such a circuit requires cross-country travel between the canyons and may entail substantial bushwhacking in the upper reaches of Little Dominguez.

Waterfall in Big Dominguez Canyon, Dominguez Canyon Wilderness Study Area. John Fielder photograph.

Mark Pearson

16   GRANITE CREEK

Location:	30 miles southwest of Grand Junction
Elevation Range:	4,600 – 7,600 feet
Vegetation/Ecosystem:	Piñon-juniper; cottonwood-boxelder riparian zone
Roadless Acreage:	9,520 acres
Wilderness Status:	Not proposed for wilderness by BLM
Special Features:	Perennial stream; slickrock canyon
USGS Maps:	Coates Creek (15'), Two V Basin

Granite Creek is a lush, red sandstone canyon tributary of the Dolores River. The canyon, ranging in depth to 800 feet, is dotted with picturesque fins, columns, windows and buttes. The higher-elevation eastern end of Granite Creek Canyon is relatively open and straight, whereas the western end of the canyon where it joins the Dolores River is so serpentine that the stream runs seven miles to cover three horizontal miles.

Granite Creek begins amid piñon-juniper and oakbrush benches on the extreme northwest edge of the Uncompahgre Plateau in an area called the

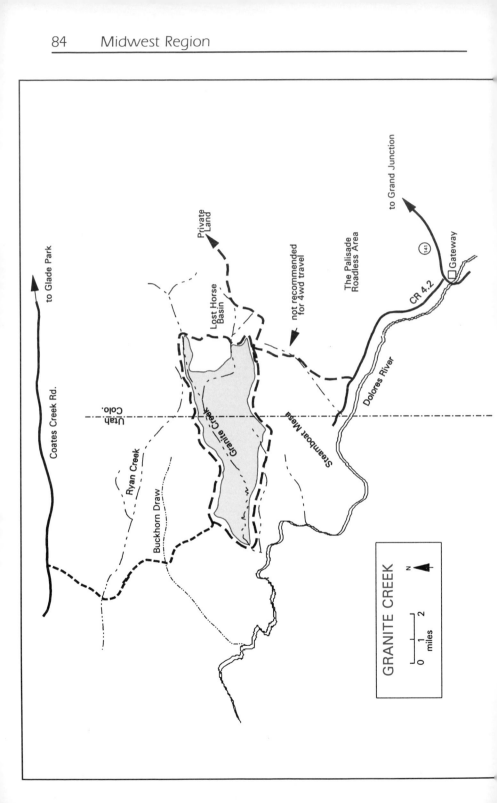

GRANITE CREEK

N

0   1   2
     miles

to Grand Junction

Gateway

141

CR 4.2

The Palisade
Roadless Area

Dolores River

not recommended
for 4wd travel

Private
Land

Lost Horse
Basin

Steamboat Mesa

Granite Creek

Utah
Colo.

to Glade Park

Coates Creek Rd.

Ryan Creek

Buckhorn Draw

Dolores Triangle. The Dolores Triangle is one of the most remote and unvisited corners of Colorado and consists of the triangle of land between the Colorado and Dolores rivers along the Colorado-Utah line. Spectacular views of the river canyons and the snow-capped La Sal Mountains are gained from canyon rims, but down below perennial Granite Creek creates a lush riparian habitat that includes cottonwoods and boxelders.

An intriguing and extremely scenic access to Granite Creek is from the Dolores River canyon downstream of Gateway. From Gateway, follow County Road 4 2/10 six miles on the north side of the river to a rough track that parallels a fence line running north. This track ultimately climbs 2,000 feet in perilous fashion until it reaches a fault that provides a break in the Wingate Sandstone cliffs. The track is often impassable to vehicles (maybe even when it is in premium condition!) but makes for a splendid hike. Upon reaching the top of the cliffs, take the left branch of the road, pass through an old burn and branch right to a road that forms the perimeter of the Granite Creek roadless area. From this road, several routes can be found into the westward-trending canyon. A primitive road provides an easy hiking route through the canyon bottom.

Granite Creek may be also reached from Grand Junction via Glade Park. From Grand Junction, drive through the Colorado National Monument to Glade Park and follow the road approximately 30 miles west, across the state line into Utah. At this point, the road branches to the left and heads to the Dolores River ford above Dewey Bridge, Utah. Follow the road three miles or so south; then branch back east along another road that in five-to-six miles will take you to the rim of Granite Creek. A miner has bulldozed a road down the cliffs to the canyon bottom, and this road defines the downstream boundary of the roadless area. From here, it is an arduous 10-mile hike up the canyon to the state line.

As a tributary of the Dolores River, Granite Creek is easily accessible by boat (when the Dolores has water). The stretch of the Dolores River between Gateway and Dewey Bridge receives little recreational use and includes at least one challenging rapid (Stateline) as well as several beautiful desert canyons. Granite Creek is a major canyon on the north bank of the river. The roadless section of the canyon begins only a mile upstream from the Dolores River and is well worth a side trip for boaters.

John Fielder

17   GUNNISON GORGE

Location:	10 miles northeast of Montrose
Elevation Range:	5,400 – 8,200 feet
Vegetation/Ecosystem:	Piñon-juniper; sagebrush; cottonwood-boxelder
Roadless Acreage:	21,038 acres
Wilderness Status:	21,038 acres proposed for wilderness by BLM
Special Features:	Gunnison River; trout fishery
USGS Maps:	Black Ridge, Red Rock Canyon

Gunnison Gorge consists of the 13 miles of the Gunnison River downstream of the Black Canyon of the Gunnison National Monument. Three basic geographic features define the Gunnison Gorge — a sheer inner river gorge, a slightly broader outer gorge and rolling uplands.

The inner gorge consists of Precambrian schist and gneiss, dissected by intrusive pegmatite dikes. Riparian vegetation, including boxelder, cottonwood and stands of exotic tamarisk, are found along the river. The Gunnison River

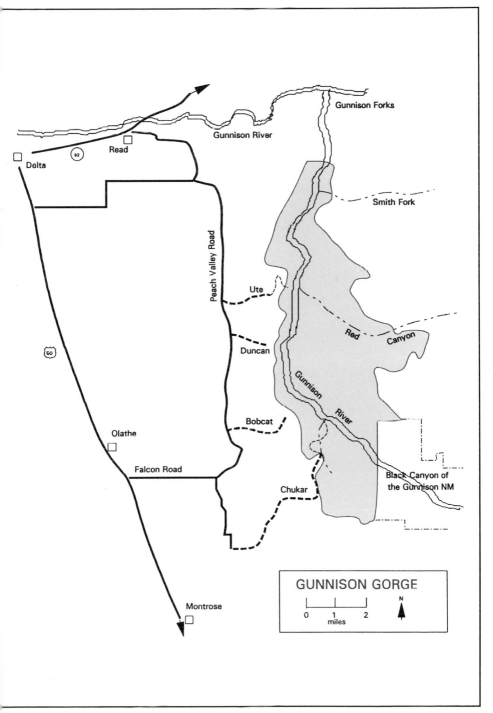

Gunnison Forks

Gunnison River

Read

Delta

Smith Fork

Peach Valley Road

Ute

Duncan

Red

Canyon

Gunnison

River

Bobcat

Olathe

Falcon Road

Chukar

Black Canyon of
the Gunnison NM

Montrose

GUNNISON GORGE

0   1   2
miles

N

through this section gained great popularity during the 1980s among both commercial and private rafting and kayaking enthusiasts. High water flows, generally during spring runoff, draw whitewater boaters. The more dominant appeal, however, is the gold medal trout fishery that has reestablished itself since the upstream construction of Blue Mesa Reservoir. Of national renown, this fishery draws thousands of anglers annually down one of several access trails and supplies commercial fishing guides with business well into the fall.

Although water impoundment proposals that would inundate much of the gorge have been considered for decades, two water rights holders (Colorado-Ute Electric Association and the City of Delta) are negotiating to exchange their conditional water rights for decreed rights in Blue Mesa Reservoir upstream from the area or to transfer their rights to other locations downstream from the proposed wilderness. A third water rights holder (Pittsburg & Midway) has donated a portion of its water rights for instream-flow purposes. Meanwhile, the river through the Gunnison Gorge is a congressionally designated study river that has been recommended by the National Park Service and BLM for Wild designation under the federal Wild and Scenic Rivers Act.

A broad multicolored canyon flares outward from the inner canyon rim, creating in effect a double canyon. The rock strata are colorful blends of red, buff, lavender, green and gray sedimentary rock layers. Red Canyon cuts the outer gorge laterally at its midpoint, leaving a hanging canyon gaping above the river. Its magnificently colored walls contort and fold repeatedly. The Colorado Division of Wildlife has recently reestablished bighorn sheep populations in the upper gorge.

Four trails lead into the gorge from its western ridge. In order from south to north, these are the Chukar, Bobcat, Duncan, and Ute trails. All of the trails are reached via the Peach Valley Road, which parallels the gorge. To find the Peach Valley Road from the north, either head east from Delta on a farm road or leave Highway 50 at the hamlet of Read and head south. Several miles south, a rough road climbs steeply to the Gunnison Gorge rim. The Ute Trail begins at the picnic area on the rim and drops two or three miles into Gunnison Gorge at Ute Park. Hikers wishing to spend the night will find several choice campsites in the grassy meadows and piñon-juniper stands along the river.

The Duncan and Bobcat trails similarly descend into the canyon from the rim. Turnoffs to these trails occur several miles south of the Ute Trail along the Peach Valley Road. The Peach Valley Road is a good passenger car road in dry weather. During rainstorms, however, it can turn into an impassable mudslick. The spur roads from the Peach Valley Road to the rim trailheads are steep and rocky and require a four-wheel-drive vehicle.

The Chukar Trail, the most heavily used trail, is the boat launch access and requires boaters to carry their craft 1.5 miles to the river's edge from the trail head. The river through the gorge has many Class II and Class III rapids that increase in technicality as the water level drops to occasional lows of 300 cfs. Be sure to contact the BLM office in Montrose before attempting to float the gorge.

Lack of road access helps control river use, although horse packers are available for hire to portage gear. The Chukar Trail actually approaches the gorge from the south, after a rather circuitous route south out of Peach Valley.

The closest highway access to the Chukar Trail is from Olathe where you turn east onto Falcon Road a mile south of town. At appropriate water levels, it is possible to hike upriver a couple of miles into the Black Canyon of the Gunnison National Monument from the Chukar Trail.

The eastern side of Gunnison Gorge is more gentle than the west and is shaped by broad ridges and wide valleys. Aged juniper trees create wide canopies above thick grassy spots, providing ideal campsites and respites from the intense summer sun. Mule deer and cottontail rabbits abound on these uplands. Access to the eastern uplands is gained from Highway 92 near Crawford.

Gunnison Gorge, Gunnison Gorge Wilderness Study Area. John Fielder photograph.

Mark Pearson

18   HUNTER CANYON

Location:	10 miles northwest of Grand Junction
Elevation Range:	5,400 – 8,100 feet
Vegetation/Ecosystem:	Piñon-juniper; mountain-mahogany; Douglas-fir
Roadless Acreage:	14,300 acres
Wilderness Status:	Not proposed for wilderness by BLM
Special Features:	Narrow canyons; riparian zone
USGS Maps:	Corcoran Peak

Hunter Canyon is an area of striking contrasts, ranging from narrow, serpentine canyons snaking onto the plains of the Grand Valley to lofty, chalk-colored cliffs that form a lofty escarpment at the headwaters of the area. Hunter Canyon spans a continuous range of ecosystems from the arid desert of the Grand Valley to relatively lush Douglas-fir forests in adjacent upland mesas.

Hunter Canyon itself carves a deep, winding canyon of a type uncommon in the Book Cliffs of western Colorado. The canyon breaks through the sheer, cliff-forming Mesa Verde Formation and out onto the Grand Valley in an

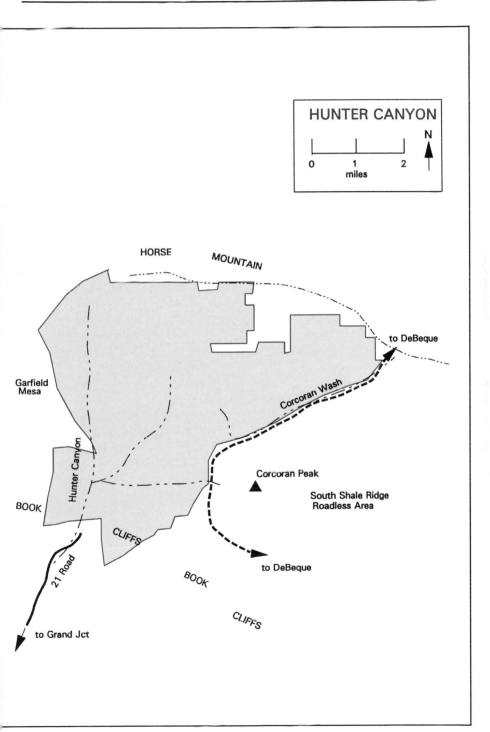

HUNTER CANYON

N

0   1   2
miles

HORSE   MOUNTAIN

to DeBeque

Garfield
Mesa

Corcoran Wash

Hunter Canyon

Corcoran Peak

South Shale Ridge
Roadless Area

BOOK

CLIFFS

21 Road

to DeBeque

BOOK

CLIFFS

to Grand Jct

abrupt fashion. The stream undercuts the rock walls, creating narrow defiles in the canyon's upper reaches, one of which can be waded to a point beneath a towering waterfall. Large, isolated ponderosa pines line the canyon bottom, providing welcome shade in the noonday summer sun.

The deep, silent canyon gives way to high mesas covered by sage, mountain-mahogany and piñon-juniper forest. Moving higher, nearing the 8,400-foot mark, the area evolves into rolling forests and gentle canyons, ultimately culminating in an escarpment of chalk-white cliffs of the Green River Formation, which creates a dramatic backdrop to Hunter Canyon. These wetter, higher elevations provide evidence of increased vegetative vigor in the form of Douglas-fir, aspen and flowering shrubs.

To reach Hunter Canyon, drive west from Grand Junction on Highways 6 and 50, past the I-70 interchange, to 21 Road. Follow 21 Road north through the irrigated farm country, cross the Highline Canal and drive another seven miles across the desert to the face of the Book Cliffs. An oil and gas access road has been bladed in the bottom of Hunter Canyon in recent years, so leave your vehicle where convenient and continue up the canyon on foot. The Middle Fork branches east a couple of miles into the canyon. This fork twists and turns as it ascends past undercut banks and small pourovers. Both the main stem and the Middle Fork are populated by Douglas-fir and scattered ponderosa pine. There is running water in both streams during the spring.

John Fielder

19   LITTLE BOOKCLIFFS

Location:	Five miles northeast of Grand Junction
Elevation Range:	5,000 – 7,300 feet
Vegetation/Ecosystem:	Piñon-juniper; greasewood; sagebrush
Roadless Acreage:	26,525 acres
Wilderness Status:	Not proposed for wilderness by BLM
Special Features:	1,000-foot deep Main Canyon; Book Cliffs escarpment; hoodoos; perennial streams
USGS Maps:	Cameo, Round Mountain, Winter Flats

Little Bookcliffs encompasses the stunning cliffs and canyons of the east end of the Book Cliffs. Thousand-foot canyon walls rise from the entrance to Main Canyon at its confluence with the Colorado River, and portions of the 2,000-foot vertical face of the Book Cliffs that frame the Grand Valley are incorporated into the area. The sheer enormity of these unscalable walls, combined with the unparalleled views from the mesas above them, creates an incomparable wilderness experience.

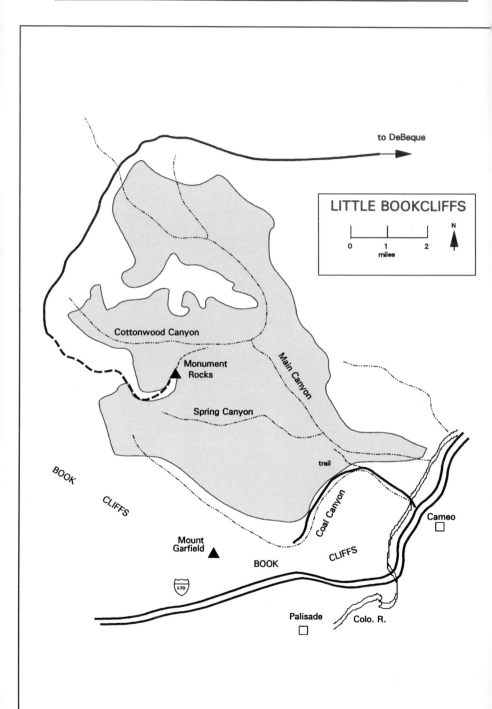

The roadless area includes two-thirds of the Little Bookcliffs Wild Horse Range, one of BLM's few officially designated Wild Horse Ranges in the United States. The 65 to 120 wild horses that roam the area are most frequently seen in Coal Canyon and Main Canyon; they offer unique subjects for observation and photography while hiking, backpacking or horseback riding. Portions of Little Bookcliffs are also critical winter range for mule deer.

Little Bookcliffs is one of very few remaining roadless areas in the Book Cliffs region of west central Colorado. The area is atypical of wilderness in Colorado, owing to its deep canyons and rolling, forested piñon-juniper mesas. Four major canyons cut through the area — Main, Cottonwood, Spring and Coal. These twisting canyons contain trickling desert streams graced by cool cottonwoods and Douglas-firs in their upper reaches. Plunge pools and water-falls are abundant in the canyons. Several natural bridges and numerous pinnacles ("hoodoos") dot the tan and gray canyon walls.

I-70 provides easy access to all of the major canyons in Little Bookcliffs. Take the Cameo exit on I-70, cross the Colorado River and drive directly past the Public Service power plant. Follow the only legal road beyond the power plant (the others are indicated by No Trespassing signs) up the mouth of Coal Canyon. The canyon will veer westward in approximately 1.5 miles, and at this point there is a cattle guard across the road. Park in the obvious cleared parking area just before the cattle guard and below a road cut into the low ridge that separates Coal Canyon from Main Canyon.

Tamarisk in October, Main Canyon, Little Bookcliffs Wilderness Study Area. John Fielder photograph.

Main Canyon is the heart of the Little Bookcliffs roadless area. From the parking area, either follow the road cut over the ridge to Main Canyon or find one of the horse trails just west of the road cut that also takes you into Main Canyon. The four-wheel-drive trail that traverses the lower reaches of Main Canyon makes for an easy hiking route. Spring Creek enters from the west a couple of miles up the canyon. Spring Creek is graced by a staggering selection of hoodoos; it gradually narrows as you ascend. A tributary on the right quickly dead-ends in an alkaline alcove; Spring Creek itself turns into a U-shaped slickrock funnel through which flows a thin skiff of water.

Farther along Main Canyon, beyond Spring Creek, several lonely cottonwoods have taken root, and the beginnings of giant alcoves appear high on the canyon walls. The canyon splits about three miles beyond Spring Creek, the right branch continuing another six or seven miles to its source tributaries, such as Alkali Canyon, and the left branch heading west as Cottonwood Canyon. A horse trail in Cottonwood Canyon ascends to Monument Rocks, a primitive BLM picnic area and campground that can be reached over dirt roads via the town of DeBeque and the Winter Flats road.

The corral pattern of the canyons in Little Bookcliffs allows for a series of multiday backpacks. It is relatively easy to scramble out of any of the canyons, and the piñon-juniper forests on the intervening plateaus do not pose a significant obstacle to cross-country travel. A hiker could spend five days hiking the length of Main Canyon, crossing Round Mountain into Cottonwood Canyon, and then climbing out to Monument Rocks and returning to Main Canyon via Spring Creek. There is running water most of the year in these canyons, though it may be high in alkali and is likely to be polluted by the wild horses.

John Fielder

20 THE PALISADE

Location:	50 miles southwest of Grand Junction
Elevation Range:	4,500–9,400 feet
Vegetation/Ecosystem:	Blackbrush desert; piñon-juniper; cottonwood; ponderosa pine; oakbrush; aspen
Roadless Acreage:	26,050 acres
Wilderness Status:	Not proposed for wilderness by BLM
Special Features:	Dolores River canyon; shale hoodoos; The Palisade; Unaweep Seep; Unaweep Canyon rim
USGS Maps:	Coates Creek (15'), Fish Creek, Gateway, Polar Mesa (15'), Two V Basin

The Palisade sits astride the edge of the Uncompahgre Uplift, forming an ecological bridge between the red slickrock tributaries of the Dolores River and the lush aspen and ponderosa forests of Unaweep Canyon. Unaweep

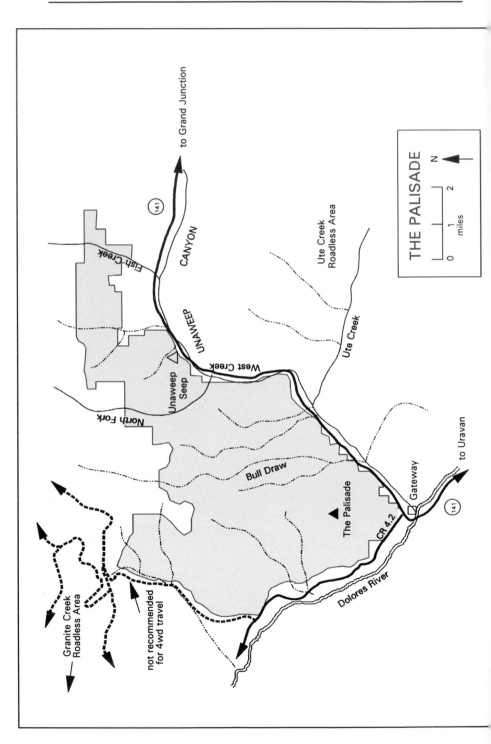

THE PALISADE

N

0   1   2
    miles

Canyon is a broad U-shaped canyon carved deep into the Uncompahgre Plateau by the ancient Gunnison and Colorado rivers. The walls of Unaweep Canyon, composed of stark black and gray schists, gneiss and granite, tower to heights of 4,000 feet above the canyon floor. This great relief is the cause of The Palisade's most outstanding feature: its wide diversity of character. Rainfall ranges from much less than 10 inches per year to more than 30. As expected, plant and animal life also vary in accordance with this diversity; few places offer such a wide range of natural characteristics over so small an area.

The western portion of The Palisade is a barren basin of low relief cut through the Chinle and Wingate formations along the Dolores River. At the edges of the basin, on all sides, are numerous hoodoos — standing columns of soft shale capped by rocks of a more resistant nature. The shale is a literal rainbow of color, predominantly milky blue, but also tinted in places with green or purple and capped with red or brown stains. Springs feed two permanent streams in this area, giving rise to delightful strings of pools and waterfalls graced by stately cottonwoods. The benchlands are dominated by blackbrush, a low desert shrub with sparse gray-green leaves, and scattered piñon pines and juniper.

Access to this portion is the same as that described for Granite Creek. Take County Road 4 2/10 north from Gateway; the four-wheel-drive trail described for Granite Creek forms the western boundary of The Palisade.

The Palisade itself is a narrow fin of sandstone surrounded on all sides by vertical walls of Wingate Sandstone and capped with the carved slickrock of the Entrada. Stands of Douglas-fir dot the shaded north slopes of this fin, and hoodoos line its western slopes. Imposing as it appears, The Palisade can be climbed. The Grand Junction group of the Colorado Mountain Club has described a route that begins on the west side from a dirt road 3.7 miles along County Road 4 2/10. Head for the most logical rib to the base of cliffs that are broken down, climb a series of ledges and traverse northerly following cairns, flagging, ropes and wires. Avoid the last cliff band by traversing south and scrambling over the sandstone dome. Head north across The Palisade to a chimney, which leads to more scrambling before reaching the summit. A rope is likely required for belay and confidence.

The eastern boundary of The Palisade runs along West Creek at the lower end of Unaweep Canyon and exists in stark contrast to the Dolores River desert to the west. Lush stands of cottonwoods grace the creek below towering black cliffs. Forests of ponderosa pine lead upward, giving way to piñon-juniper, oakbrush and ultimately aspen. Unaweep Seep sits perched on the northwest bank of West Creek. The seep — the collective name for a number of springs — creates an outstanding natural botanical display, one listed on the register of Colorado State Natural Areas. The combination of cool summer air, long growing season due to the relatively low elevation and abundant moisture leads to an astounding abundance and variety of plants. Relatively uncommon species such as groundcherry and blackberry occur here, and more prosaic species, notably boxelder, alder and smooth sumac, reach unusual size. The seep is an obvious feature that appears at the highway bridge approximately 10 miles east of Gateway.

The roadless area encompasses many miles of the rim of Unaweep Canyon. Out of sight and hearing of the ranches on the plateau above, and towering some 3,000 feet above the canyon floor below, the rim (and especially the ledge topping the precambrian granitic cliffs) appears to be related to neither. Stands of aspen adorn the rim. The rugged cliffs along either side of the canyon make this one of the most photogenic places in Colorado. At the far eastern end of the rim, Fish Creek tumbles down a spectacular series of waterfalls, dropping 1,700 feet in 1.5 miles. The rim can be reached via the North Fork of West Creek, an obvious drainage 1.5 miles downstream of the Unaweep Seep, or via Bull Draw Basin. Bull Draw Basin includes several drainages on the east side of The Palisade, beginning a couple of miles east of Gateway on Highway 141. Any of these routes requires a steep scramble through brush and piñon-juniper to the rim.

Unaweep Seep, edge of The Palisade Wilderness Study Area. John Fielder photograph.

John Fielder

21   ROUBIDEAU

Location:	15 miles west of Montrose
Elevation Range:	5,300 – 7,000 feet
Vegetation/Ecosystem:	Cottonwood riparian; sagebrush; piñon-juniper; oakbrush
Roadless Acreage:	30,680 acres (includes 20,000 acres of Forest Service land)
Wilderness Status:	Not proposed for wilderness by BLM
Special Features:	Ecological transition; perennial stream
USGS Maps:	Camel Back, Roubideau

Roubideau Creek has carved one of Colorado's most unusual canyons. Named for French fur trapper Antoine Robidoux, the canyon originates in subalpine spruce and aspen forests high on the Uncompahgre Plateau before it flows 20 miles north to the Gunnison River. Roubideau Creek's upper reaches are characterized by a small native cutthroat trout fishery and numerous beaver ponds.

As it flows northward, Roubideau Creek cuts down into Mesozoic sandstone draped over the dome of the Uncompahgre Uplift. Dakota, Morrison, Entrada

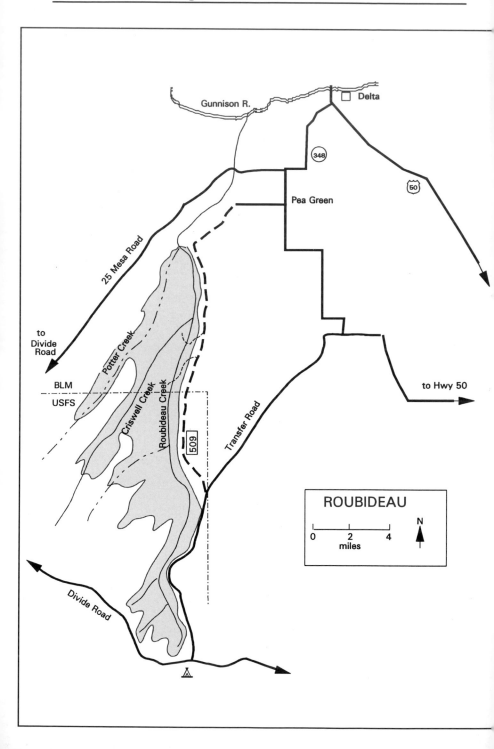

and Chinle strata form cliffs of warm colors that tower over the lush montane riparian ecosystem in the canyon bottom. This stretch of Roubideau is rich in wildlife, such as black bear, deer, bobcat, cougar and golden eagles. A great number of birds nest in the canyon, including cliff swallows, white-throated swifts, Cooper's hawks, titmice, warblers and many more.

As it flows down out of the spruce and aspen forests onto BLM lands, the canyon regime becomes more arid with rock buttresses, free-standing hoodoos, piñon and juniper and a meandering stream lined with cottonwoods. This striking lower desert canyon with its brilliant red bands of Entrada Sandstone comprises BLM's Camel Back Wilderness Study Area, so named for the large, isolated mesa between Roubideau Creek and Criswell Creek.

Approximately two-thirds of the roadless area lies on the Uncompahgre National Forest and one-third on BLM. A number of trails lead into the Forest Service portion, but the hikes described here are located in the downstream, more arid, BLM-managed area.

Two trails lead into lower Roubideau Canyon from the east canyon rim. The Transfer Road leads most directly from the Uncompahgre Valley to the canyon rim. Take Highway 348 west from Olathe (north of Montrose) and turn south in about three miles. In another four miles, National Forest access signs will direct you to the Transfer Road. As the road nears the National Forest boundary, turn north onto Forest Road 509 and follow it approximately eight miles to the BLM-Forest boundary. A primitive trail is marked by a rough sign shortly past the boundary. This trail drops into Roubideau Canyon near Ben Lowe's cabin and homestead, which is situated on private property. Once in the canyon bottom, the vegetation thins as you travel downstream. Roubideau Creek is a perennial stream with a substantial spring runoff.

A second trail, this one a stock trail, descends into the canyon another three or four miles north along the rim road. The road, although not steep, is extremely rocky and may require a high-clearance vehicle. The stock trail drops into the canyon at a point just above the confluence of Roubideau and Criswell creeks. The trail climbs out of the canyon onto the north end of Camel Back mesa. The canyon bottom at this point is characterized by sparse vegetation and scattered cottonwoods, and it is easy to travel up or down canyon at your leisure. A 30-foot tall hoodoo composed of multicolored sediments sits a short distance up the west slope of the canyon.

A road leads into the mouth of the canyon at the north end of the roadless area and offers an access point for hikes up the canyon. Vegetation is sparsest in this lowest, most arid stretch of the canyon. From the center of Delta, follow the National Forest access signs to the Twenty-Five Mesa road. Just after crossing Roubideau Creek, a dirt road branches south. The road turns into Potter Canyon in about five miles. Leave your vehicle here and head up Roubideau Canyon on foot.

Mark Pearson

22   SEWEMUP MESA

Location:	15 miles south of Gateway
Elevation Range:	4,900 –7,500 feet
Vegetation/Ecosystem:	Piñon-juniper; ponderosa pine; mountain-mahogany
Roadless Acreage:	30,385 acres (includes 9,500 acres of Forest Service land)
Wilderness Status:	18,835 acres proposed for wilderness by BLM
Special Features:	Sinbad Valley cliffs; Roc Creek Canyon; ponderosa pine forest; La Sal Mountain views
USGS Maps:	Juanita Arch, La Sal (15'), Polar Mesa (15'), Roc Creek

Sewemup Mesa is one of the most ecologically pristine areas in Colorado, owing to the isolation imposed by its almost impassable belt of encircling sandstone cliffs. Perhaps the greatest single wilderness value of Sewemup Mesa

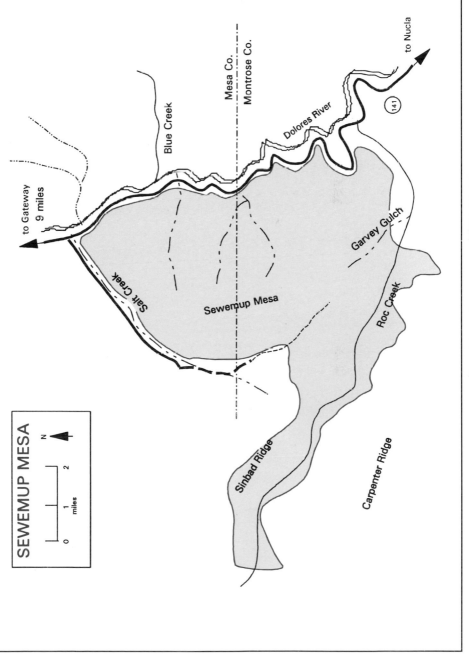

is the fact that the mesa has been left ungrazed by domestic livestock, providing an example of an ecosystem largely undisturbed by human activities.

A striking feature of Sewemup Mesa is its band of thousand-foot-high cliffs of Wingate Sandstone enclosing more than three-quarters of the area. To the east, these cliffs rise out of the sheer slickrock gorge of the Dolores River, and to the west they tower above Sinbad Valley, the remnants of a collapsed salt dome. Domes of pink banded Entrada Sandstone dot the top of the mesa, breaking the sloping landscape of piñon-juniper forest. Many huge ponderosa pines line the canyons of the mesa top and grow directly from sandstone terraces along the mesa's western cliffs. Few places offer such exhilarating solitude, as well as spectacular views of Sinbad Valley and the La Sal Mountains, as can be obtained from the edge of Sewemup Mesa's boundless cliffs.

In contrast to the towering heights of Sewemup Mesa, adjacent Roc Creek Canyon plummets 1,000 feet in the opposite direction — straight down, forming an imposing cleft between Sinbad and Carpenter ridges. Roc Creek forms the largest canyon draining east from the La Sal Mountains. Its red walls are framed by forests of Douglas-fir and ponderosa pine along the canyon rims. Roc Creek itself is a large, roaring creek lined with huge ponderosas.

Sewemup Mesa derives its name from the cattle rustling exploits of the McCarty Gang. Adjacent Roc Creek, Sinbad Ridge and Sinbad Valley are named for Sinbad the Sailor and the giant bird, the legendary roc, as chronicled in *A Thousand and One Arabian Nights*.

There are a couple of routes from Highway 141 into Sewemup Mesa. Take the highway approximately 15 miles south from Gateway; immediately beyond the Montrose-Mesa county line a large canyon meets the highway. The first mile or so of this canyon is very rugged hiking, but once a low alcove is passed, it is possible to climb out of the canyon to easier traveling through piñon-juniper and ponderosa pine forests. The mesa dips significantly from west to east, so it is a continuous upward climb three miles across the width of the mesa to the top of the 2,000-foot cliffs that define the western perimeter of the mesa. Small potholes dot the mesa top, providing an occasional source of water, and running streams may be encountered in the shallow canyons that crisscross the mesa.

Another route onto Sewemup from the highway departs near the southern edge of the mesa, just north of the Roc Creek drainage. The mesa is broken down at this point, and it is possible to scramble up the ledges and talus onto the rim of the mesa.

The mouth of Roc Creek is in private ownership, and permission will be required to hike up Roc Creek Canyon from its mouth. Alternatively, it is possible to drop into Roc Creek from Sewemup Mesa. The southwest corner of the mesa slopes into a saddle where it connects with Sinbad Ridge. Hikers can take Garvey Gulch down into Roc Creek from here, skirting private land, or can follow Sinbad Ridge several miles west to the upper reaches of Roc Creek where the canyon walls are less imposing. The saddle is reached either by crossing the mesa, beginning at the highway, or through Sinbad Valley. Much of Sinbad Valley is also privately owned, and permission may be required to use this route.

October snowfall, Sewemup Mesa Wilderness Study Area. John Fielder photograph.

Mark Pearson

23   SOUTH SHALE RIDGE

Location:	18 miles northeast of Grand Junction
Elevation Range:	5,200 – 8,100 feet
Vegetation/Ecosystem:	Piñon-juniper; ponderosa and Douglas-fir
Roadless Acreage:	31,391 acres
Wilderness Status:	Not proposed for wilderness by BLM
Special Features:	Hoodoos (Goblin Valley); colorful badlands; sweeping vistas
USGS Maps:	Corcoran Peak, Wagon Track Ridge, Winter Flats

Portions of South Shale Ridge might easily be called Colorado's Bryce Canyon. The south face of the ridge is a steep, multicolored escarpment of vivid purples, oranges and reds. Towering Douglas-firs grace the landscape at the west end of the area, providing a refreshing highlight to the stark terrain of the ridge itself.

South Shale Ridge is a highly eroded feature of the colorful Wasatch Formation, ranging in elevation from 5,200 feet at its eastern base to 8,076 feet on

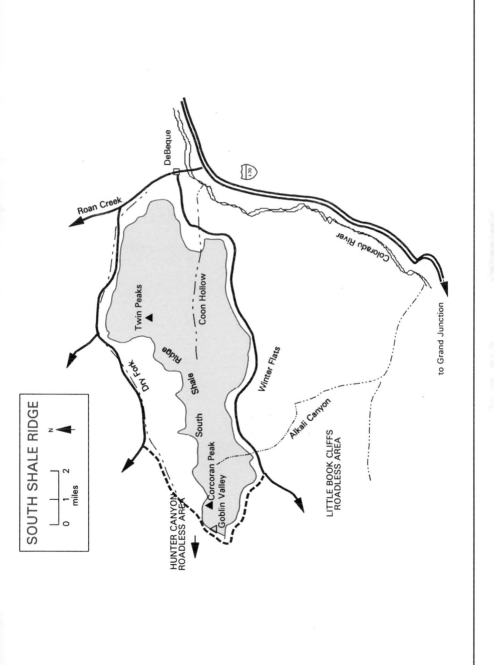

SOUTH SHALE RIDGE

N

0   1   2
miles

DeBeque

Roan Creek

I-70

Colorado River

to Grand Junction

Twin Peaks

Coon Hollow

Dry Fork

South Shale Ridge

Winter Flats

Alkali Canyon

Corcoran Peak

Goblin Valley

HUNTER CANYON
ROADLESS AREA

LITTLE BOOK CLIFFS
ROADLESS AREA

the summit of Corcoran Peak. Over 40 miles of twisting arroyos carve through this rugged landscape, often opening into secluded parks at their sources.

A number of outstanding special features complement the area's rugged beauty. Goblin Valley is a ghostly collection of white and gray hoodoos guarding the western flank of the ridge. Several rare and endangered plants grow in or near South Shale Ridge. The threatened cactus *Sclerocactus glaucus* is known to exist within the unit, and the rare *Phacelia submutica* is suspected to occur there as well. In addition, Pyramid Rock Research Natural Area, which is just across the road from South Shale Ridge, was designated to protect the endangered Uinta Basin hookless cactus.

Hikers enjoy sweeping vistas of the Grand Mesa, the San Juan Mountains, the La Sal Mountains and the scenic ridge lines of the Roan Cliffs from the crest of South Shale Ridge. Raptors soar on air currents swirling above the ridge, and deer frequent the slopes and valleys of the area.

To reach South Shale Ridge, exit I-70 at the town of DeBeque, approximately 30 miles east of Grand Junction. Drive to the southwest corner of the town and find the county road to Winter Flats. This road heads directly west for a couple of miles before skirting the south flank of South Shale Ridge. There are no trails in South Shale Ridge, but the open nature of its badlands topography allows for easy cross-country travel anywhere along its length. The south-draining arroyos offer many routes to the ridge top and contain fantastic colors and shapes. If you follow the road the entire length of the ridge to its western extent, it ultimately gains elevation and passes through a magical forest of stately Douglas-firs scattered across red, pink and orange badlands. Corcoran Peak, the high point in the area at 8,076 feet, can be scaled from this western terminus of the ridge. Goblin Valley lies along the road on the extreme western boundary of the roadless area, just west of Corcoran Peak.

Mark Pearson

24   UTE CREEK

Location:	Six miles northeast of Gateway
Elevation Range:	5,600 – 9,400 feet
Vegetation/Ecosystem:	Piñon-juniper; oakbrush; ponderosa pine; aspen
Roadless Acreage:	44,000 acres (includes 35,000 acres of Forest Service land)
Wilderness Status:	Not proposed for wilderness by BLM
Special Features:	Aspen forests; scenic vistas
USGS Maps:	Casto Reservoir, Fish Creek, Pine Mountain

Ute Creek consists of the steep granite cliffs of Unaweep Canyon, 1,000-foot-deep Ute Creek Canyon and surrounding gently sloping mesa tops at the north end of the Uncompahgre Plateau. The area is highly representative of southwestern Colorado's scenic canyons, piñon-juniper forests and groves of aspen and spruce. The roadless area includes 9,000 acres of BLM lands and approximately 35,000 acres of National Forest lands.

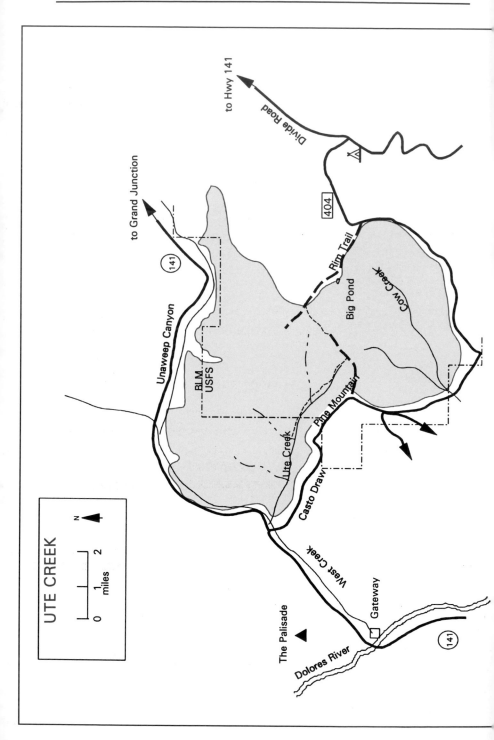

UTE CREEK

N

0   1   2
miles

to Hwy 141

Divide Road

to Grand Junction

404

Rim Trail

Big Pond

Cow Creek

141

Unaweep Canyon

BLM
USFS

Pine Mountain

Ute Creek

Casto Draw

West Creek

The Palisade

Gateway

Dolores River

141

The roadless area includes the deepest and most dramatic portions of Unaweep Canyon, reaching depths of 2,000 to 3,300 feet. A number of steep canyons, such as Ute Creek, drain the Uncompahgre Plateau as they cut through the area. A piñon-juniper forest blankets much of this rugged terrain, and thick riparian growth characterizes the drainage bottoms, ranging from willows and cottonwoods to ponderosa pine, Douglas-fir and oakbrush. The rolling mesa tops above the rugged canyons are covered by large aspen forests broken by sagebrush flats and ringed by lush spruce forests on northern and western slopes.

The Snowshoe Trail provides relatively easy access into the heart of the roadless area. This trail leaves the top of the plateau from a four-wheel-drive road called the Rim Trail. Both trails afford spectacular views of the La Sal Mountains, Lone Cone, the Abajo Mountains and Unaweep Canyon and pass through a number of the vast aspen glades that characterize the area. To get to the Rim Trail, take Highway 141 south from Whitewater to the Divide Road, the primary Forest Service access road to the Uncompahgre Plateau. Follow the Divide Road to Divide Fork Campground and turn west on Forest Road 404 approximately three miles to Forest Road 416, or the Rim Trail, a rough four-wheel-drive road. The Snowshoe Trail drops off the plateau just beyond Big Pond, four miles up the Rim Trail.

Several routes lead into the roadless area from the west side as well. The Casto Draw road runs southwest from Highway 141 approximately five miles east of Gateway and forms the western boundary of the roadless area as it climbs across the face of Pine Mountain. The vegetation changes abruptly during this climb from saltbush desert to ponderosa pine forest. A couple of miles after cresting Pine Mountain, a four-wheel-drive track takes off east into the broad valley of Ute Creek. This track connects with the Snowshoe Trail. A faint trail might also be located that parallels Ute Creek downstream from this track.

NORTHWEST COLORADO

Opposite: Canyon scrambling, Bull Canyon Wilderness Study Area. Dave Cooper photograph.

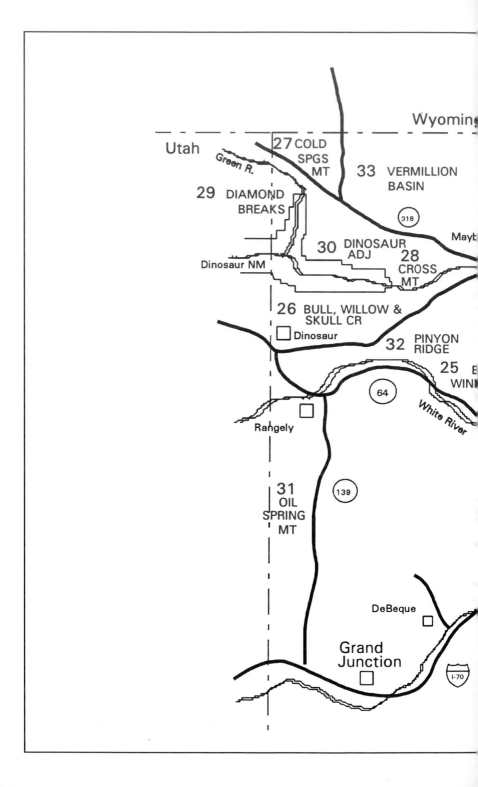

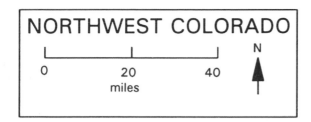

NORTHWEST COLORADO

0   20   40

miles

N

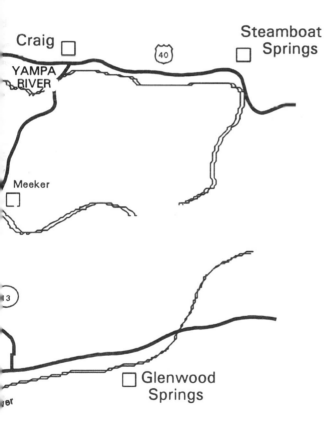

Craig

Steamboat
Springs

40

YAMPA
RIVER

Meeker

3

Glenwood
Springs

Windy Gulch, Dave Cooper

25   BLACK MOUNTAIN and WINDY GULCH

Location:	12 miles west of Meeker
Elevation Range:	6,100 – 7,205 feet
Vegetation/Ecosystem:	Sagebrush; piñon-juniper; oakbrush; Douglas-fir
Roadless Acreage:	22,206 acres
Wilderness Status:	Not proposed for wilderness by BLM
Special Features:	Big-game herds; White River frontage; raptors
USGS Maps:	Buckskin Point, White River City, White Rock

Black Mountain and Windy Gulch are two contiguous roadless areas just north of the White River and Highway 64. The areas consist of high ridge tops and steep-sided valleys with rugged walls graced by stately Douglas-firs. The southerly slopes of the areas are covered by dense piñon-juniper forest, scrub oak and serviceberry.

Both areas provide crucial wildlife habitat immediately adjacent to the Piceance

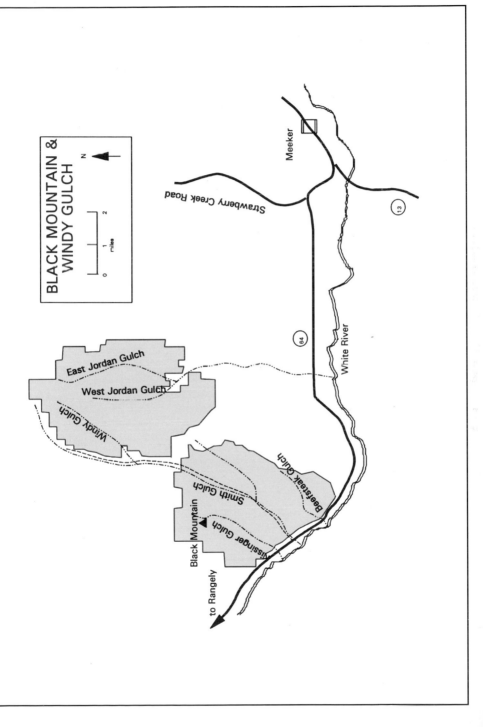

BLACK MOUNTAIN &
WINDY GULCH

N

0   1   2
miles

Meeker

Strawberry Creek Road

13

64

White River

East Jordan Gulch

West Jordan Gulch

Windy Gulch

Smith Gulch

Beefsteak Gulch

Vissinger Gulch

Black Mountain

to Rangely

Basin. All of Black Mountain, for example, sits within prime mule deer habitat, and several thousand acres are considered critical winter range for as many as 3,000 mule deer. A major mule deer migration corridor crosses Black Mountain, with up to 8,000 animals annually. The areas are also winter range for elk and year-round habitat for a small population of mountain lions.

The boundary of Black Mountain follows the White River along Highway 64 for approximately four miles. Several parallel drainages provide natural hiking routes within the area. The largest of these is Smith Gulch, which is marked by a small highway bridge and a dirt road on the west side of the gulch about 12 miles west of Meeker. A sign on the gate to this road notes that it provides legal public access to the BLM lands beyond. A four-wheel-drive track follows Smith Gulch for about four miles and traverses the entire width of the area. Approximately halfway up the canyon, a large tributary canyon branches to the east and offers additional hiking opportunities. From anywhere along the length of Smith Gulch, hikers can strike out cross-country west over a ridge to Kissinger Gulch, and make a loop trip by returning to the highway about a mile from Smith Gulch. There is no water in these drainages, however, so bring your own.

The Smith Gulch drainage also offers the best legal public access to Windy Gulch. The Windy Gulch roadless area lies immediately north of Black Mountain, and Windy Gulch is itself a tributary of Smith Gulch. Simply follow Smith Gulch six miles to its confluence with Windy Gulch; from there you can hike up Windy Gulch to its source or traverse east over a ridge to West or East Jordan gulches.

All of the drainages in the two areas contain sandstone cliffs set in dense forests of piñon-juniper, with sagebrush-covered valley floors. The cliffs offer prime nesting sites for raptors, and there are three active golden eagle nests within the Black Mountain roadless area. Bald eagles wintering in cottonwoods along the White River also frequently visit Black Mountain and Windy Gulch on hunting excursions.

Willow Creek, Dave Cooper

26 BULL CANYON, WILLOW CREEK and SKULL CREEK

Location:	One mile north of the town of Dinosaur
Elevation Range:	5,600 – 8,200 feet
Vegetation/Ecosystem:	Piñon-juniper forest; sagebrush
Roadless Acreage:	44,800 acres
Wilderness Status:	40,655 acres proposed for wilderness by BLM
Special Features:	Slickrock canyons; raptors; ancient piñon pine forests; Dominguez/Escalante Trail
USGS Maps:	Lazy Y Point, Plug Hat Rock, Skull Creek, Snake John Reef

Bull Canyon, Willow Creek and Skull Creek are three contiguous roadless areas between Highway 40 and Dinosaur National Monument. They lie along the southern flanks of Blue Mountain, an uplifted and faulted plateau at the far southeast end of the massive Uinta Mountain range. Travelers on Highway

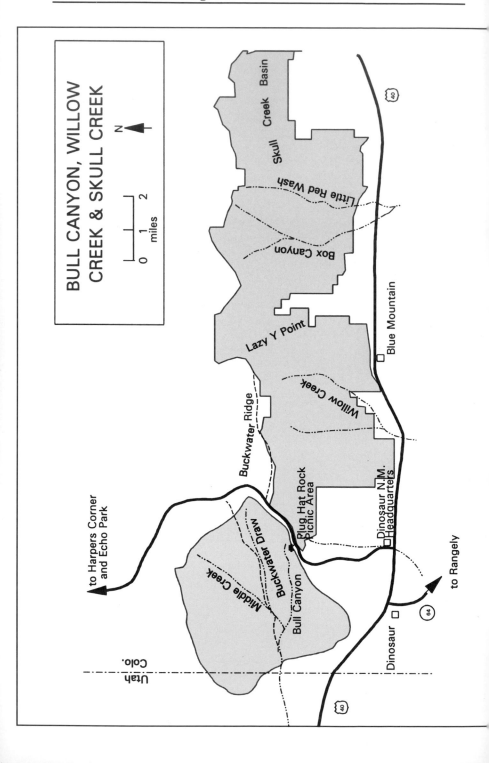

BULL CANYON, WILLOW
CREEK & SKULL CREEK

N

0 1 2
miles

Skull   Creek   Basin

Little Red Wash

Box Canyon

Lazy Y Point

Buckwater Ridge

Willow Creek

Blue Mountain

Plug Hat Rock
Picnic Area

Dinosaur N.M.
Headquarters

Middle Creek

Buckwater Draw

Bull Canyon

to Harpers Corner
and Echo Park

Utah
Colo.

Dinosaur

64

to Rangely

40

40

40 who gaze through gaps in the hogback ridge just north of the road will get a glimpse of the wild topography beyond. White sandstone flatirons stand in rows, reflecting the fierce summer sun. Colored slopes, green and purple Morrison shales and deep vermillion Triassic shales and sandstones rise beyond the flatirons. Massive pale pink outcrops of the Weber Sandstone lie above them, the same rock through which the Yampa River cuts its fantastic canyon just a few miles north in Dinosaur National Monument.

The areas provide important habitat for abundant wildlife populations. Raptor populations are perhaps most significant, including eleven active golden eagle nests, great horned owls, red-tailed hawks and marsh hawks. BLM has also identified the areas as potential peregrine falcon habitat for the falcons that frequent the National Monument.

Bull Canyon, Willow Creek and Skull Creek possess a couple of uncommon features that make them all the more interesting to explore. A documented campsite of the 1776 expedition of Dominguez and Escalante is located within the Bull Canyon roadless area, and the National Park Service has proposed the Dominguez/Escalante Trail for designation as a National Historic Trail. The areas are also home to ancient piñon pine forests that BLM believes to be among the oldest on the North American continent, dating to the twelfth century. Scientists have used the results of tree-ring studies in these forests to determine climatic variability in North America.

Bull Canyon is the westernmost of the three areas and straddles the Colorado-Utah state line. The National Park Service access road to Harpers Corner forms the eastern boundary of Bull Canyon and leads past the Plug Hat Rock picnic area, situated overlooking the brilliant white walls of Bull Canyon 3.5 miles north of the Monument headquarters. From the picnic area, it is possible to descend a steep slope and work your way around the southern rim of the canyon to the canyon floor. Bull Canyon often contains a trickle of water to tickle your toes enroute to the broad, open reaches of the lower canyon. Swinging north across this open valley takes the hiker to Buckwater Draw and an eroded four-wheel-drive trail. The trail can be followed east back up to the forested benchlands and ultimately intersects the Park Service access road several miles beyond the picnic area. Alternatively, it is possible to travel cross-country across these benchlands and intervening drainages south to the picnic area.

Willow Creek roadless area lies immediately across the road to the east of Bull Canyon. The watercourses here run north-south rather than east-west as in Bull Canyon, and the best access is found from Highway 40. A hike up Willow Creek itself offers a representative glimpse of the area. Park along Highway 40 just west of the hamlet of Blue Mountain and hike through the gap in the hogback north to the Willow Creek drainage. Willow Creek is a flat valley framed by low sandstone cliffs. As you follow the creek upward, the walls close in and short slot canyons begin to branch. The cliffs ultimately require that you scramble to continue to the higher benches north of the roadless area. Hikers can take a different route back to the highway, traveling cross-country through the piñon-juniper forest down the sloping fronts of the hogbacks.

To traverse across the benchland above Willow Creek, drive two miles past the Plug Hat Rock picnic area along the National Monument access road and park where a four-wheel-drive trail heads east. Hike east about 2.5 miles, and head south to a viewpoint overlooking Red Wash and Lazy Y Point.

Skull Creek is not physically separated from Willow Creek by any feature other than an abandoned four-wheel-drive trail, so BLM has proposed the two areas be designated wilderness as one combined unit. Skull Creek includes a portion of the Skull Creek Basin, which is eroded like a giant bite from the dome of the plateau and forms a spectacular seven-mile-long crater ringed by cliffs and hogbacks. Incised into the sides and bottom of the basin, but discernible from above only with effort and a map, are numerous slot canyons. Cutting into red sandstone, smooth green shale and finally hard white sandstone, the slot canyon of Box Creek offers an alluring introduction to the wonders of the Skull Creek roadless area. Hiking in Box Canyon, one often encounters places where the canyon walls are less than six feet apart; in other places, the walls vault upward over 600 feet.

Bull Canyon, Bull Canyon Wilderness Study Area. Eric Finstick photograph.

The entrance to Box Canyon is two miles north of Highway 40 and five miles east of Blue Mountain via County Road 165. Box Canyon is only a couple of miles in length but includes several tributary canyons. The county road takes you within a mile of the canyon mouth.

Just east of Box Canyon are Martin Gap and Red Wash. Martin Gap is a dramatic cleft in the last hogback, which creates an imposing gateway into the roadless area. Beyond Martin Gap, the creek bed follows the sweeping curve of the exposed Skull Creek anticline. The same brilliant reds, whites and greens of Box Canyon are also exposed here. Martin Gap is .75 miles off the highway and is approached via County Roads 165 and 104 (a segment of the old highway).

27   COLD SPRINGS MOUNTAIN

Location:	Immediately north of Browns Park National Wildlife Refuge, 100 miles west of Craig
Elevation Range:	5,800 – 8,600 feet
Vegetation/Ecosystem:	Piñon-juniper; sagebrush meadows and aspen; Douglas-fir
Roadless Acreage:	50,872 acres
Wilderness Status:	Not proposed for wilderness by BLM
Special Features:	Big-game herds; dramatic views; trout fishery
USGS Maps:	Beaver Basin, Big Joe Basin, Irish Canyon, Ladore School, Willow Creek Butte

Cold Springs Mountain is the tail end of the Uinta Mountain uplift in Utah and forms the northern ridge of Browns Park in extreme northwest Colorado. The mountain, rising gently from Browns Park, has a dense mantle of piñon-juniper forest. This forest gradually succumbs to sagebrush meadows and intermittent stands of aspen along the crest of the mountain. Numerous springs, from which the mountain gets its name, surface on top and support large numbers of elk, deer and antelope. The mountain offers many dramatic views of Browns Park, the Gates of Ladore in Dinosaur National Monument, the snow-covered Uintas and the abrupt slopes of Diamond Breaks immediately across the Green River.

Beaver Creek, a permanent stream that supports a population of endangered cutthroat trout, has cut a dramatic canyon in the west end of the mountain. The mouth of the canyon is the Beaver Creek unit of the Colorado Division of Wildlife's Browns Park State Wildlife Area. Hikers can gain access to Beaver Creek from Highway 318, directly across from the Browns Park National Wildlife Refuge headquarters. A locked gate prevents vehicular travel on the road in the lower end of Beaver Creek. A cattle trail provides the hiking route through the canyon. Bighorn sheep may be spotted along Beaver Creek.

Farther east, the Matt Trail climbs from the valley floor through dense piñon-juniper forest and old burns to the mountain crest. The Matt Trail is unmarked but begins approximately 4.5 miles west of the Browns Park store at a gate along Highway 318. The gate is marked by a sign prohibiting vehicular travel, and the trail is an obvious scar through the forest. The Matt Trail reaches the summit of the mountain in about four miles and leads to a primitive BLM campground atop the mountain. Road access to this campground is via

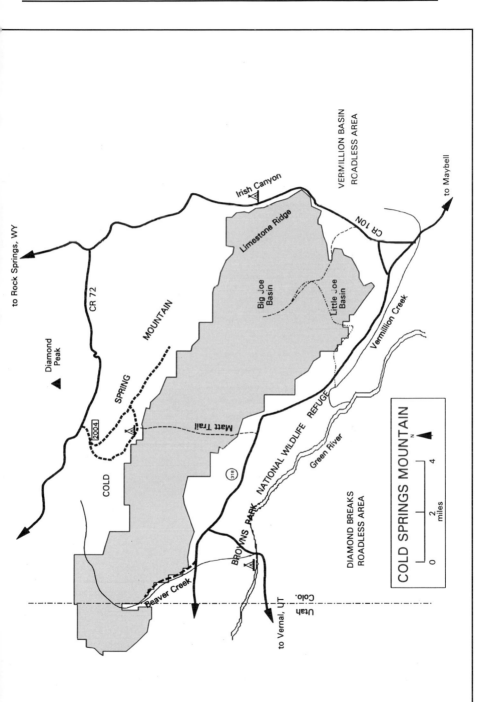

COLD SPRINGS MOUNTAIN

County Road 10N through Irish Canyon and then west on County Road 72 to the Diamond Peak area.

Limestone Ridge dominates the eastern end of the mountain. At an elevation of 8,636 feet, Limestone Ridge offers magnificent vistas, fossils, flowers, rare plant communities and an endangered plant species, *Parthenium ligulatum*. Limestone Ridge drops into spectacular Irish Canyon, where 12 geological formations representing over 600 million years of geological history are exposed. Limestone Ridge is wide-open country with no trails, and the hiker can pick one of several routes. An interesting hike can be made beginning at the mouth of Irish Canyon and following the gully immediately west up the steep hillsides to the summit of the ridge. Another hike that starts from the same location skirts west along the base of the hillside for two miles to a four-wheel-drive trail and then heads into Green Canyon and Little Joe Basin.

Matt trail, Cold Springs Mountain Wilderness Study Area. Dave Cooper photograph.

Eric Finstick

28   CROSS MOUNTAIN

Location:	45 miles west of Craig
Elevation Range:	5,600 – 7,800 feet
Vegetation/Ecosystem:	Sagebrush; piñon-juniper
Roadless Acreage:	16,760 acres
Wilderness Status:	14,981 acres proposed for wilderness by BLM
Special Features:	Cross Mountain Gorge; bighorn sheep and other big-game animals; endangered species
USGS Maps:	Elk Springs (15'), Lone Mountain (15')

Cross Mountain is a magnificent example of desert wilderness. Home to all of the major big-game animal species in Colorado and to a handful of endangered species, Cross Mountain's gorge and crest offer unmatched scenic panoramas. Other features include numerous and varied recreational opportunities ranging from Class V kayaking to caving and hunting, abundant cultural resources and educationally important landforms and strata.

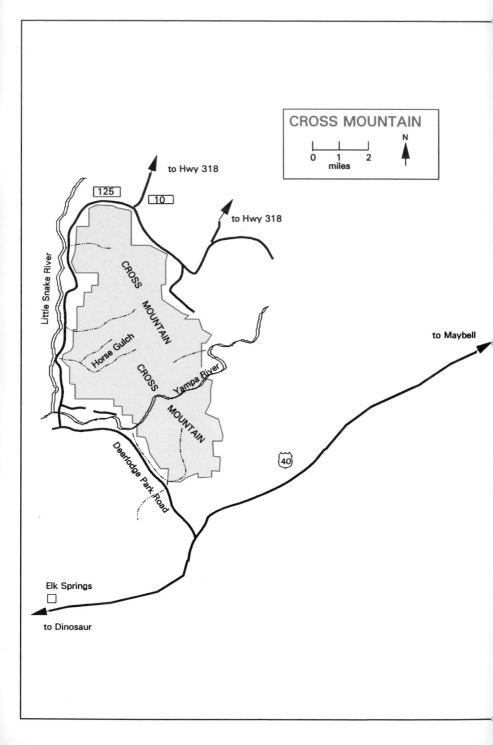

Cross Mountain is a dominant feature of the landscape, an oblong flat-topped mountain trending north and south that rises 2,200 feet above the floodplains of the Yampa and Little Snake rivers. This four-mile-wide, nine-mile-long anticlinal mountain is cleft toward its southern end by the Yampa River, resulting in a 1,200-foot-deep, sheer-walled limestone canyon.

Cross Mountain Gorge provides one of the most challenging whitewater boating experiences in the country during spring runoff and offers an ideal setting for novice boaters in late-year low water. Four species of rare, endangered fish inhabit the Yampa River through the gorge: the Colorado River squawfish, humpback chub, razorback sucker and bonytail chub. Other canyon inhabitants are bighorn sheep, bald and golden eagles and peregrine falcons.

Though only 3.5 miles long, the gorge is a full day of hiking along its rugged north river bank during low water, the only bank passable to hikers. Cross Mountain Gorge is reached from the National Park Service access road to Deerlodge Park, which leaves Highway 40 about seven or eight miles east of Elk Springs. The access road drops down to the Yampa River and intersects Moffat County Road 125 at a bridge near the confluence with the Little Snake. Travel north on CR 125 about a mile and then take a dirt track a couple of miles back east to the mouth of Cross Mountain Gorge on the north side of the Yampa River (this track is currently on private land, and you may need to obtain permission from the ranch near the intersection). The route through the gorge is a rugged scramble across talus below limestone cliffs. The entrance to the gorge provides an immediate challenge, as you must scale a short wall to get around the entrance cliffs and into the canyon. There is a decrepit rope that might be of assistance in surmounting this eight-to-10-foot obstacle. The river bank can be followed throughout almost the entire length of the canyon, but to exit the eastern end of the gorge requires that you climb the first row of cliffs prior to reaching an impassable wall at river level.

A dam was proposed by the Colorado River Water Conservation District and Colorado-Ute Electric Association in the 1970s for the western end of the canyon, and evidence of some of the exploratory work is still visible just inside the canyon's mouth. Colorado-Ute dropped its plans for the hydroelectric dam in 1983 when the economic unfeasibility of the project became apparent. However, the Colorado River Water Conservation District still hopes to build a dam, and is conducting on-going studies.

Both canyon rims offer truly spectacular views of the canyon and river. The south rim is easily accessed from the parking lot at the canyon's mouth on the south side of the river. This parking lot and viewing area are obvious along the National Park Service access road where the Yampa River first comes into view. From the parking lot, cross the fence and pick a route through the piñon-juniper forest to the rim of the canyon. The rim can be followed with few detours the entire length of the gorge. The north rim can be reached from the same point as the hike into the gorge.

The crest of Cross Mountain provides sweeping vistas of northwest Colorado; from it you are likely to sight elk, pronghorn, mule deer and perhaps wild horses. No established trails exist to the top of the mountain, but its gentle slopes allow access along its entire length on both east and west. The western side of the mountain is defined by County Road 125 and the eastern side by County Road 10, which leaves Highway 318 west of Maybell. Park anywhere along the road and climb one of the ridges or canyons to the mountain summit. The summit, only 7,800 feet, is a surprising landscape of knee-high grasses and pockets of piñon-juniper forest, though water sources are scarce. The encircling county roads allow for numerous one-way hikes across the mountain or along its length, with vehicles left at beginning and end.

Cross Mountain Gorge and the Yampa River, Cross Mountain Wilderness Study Area. Mark Pearson photograph.

Mark Pearson

DIAMOND BREAKS

Location:	On Colorado-Utah state line adjacent to Dinosaur National Monument
Elevation Range:	5,400 – 8,700 feet
Vegetation/Ecosystem:	Piñon-juniper; mountain-mahogany-oakbrush
Roadless Acreage:	41,040 acres
Wilderness Status:	36,240 acres proposed for wilderness by BLM
Special Features:	Views into Dinosaur National Monument; Browns Park
USGS Maps:	Canyon of Ladore North, Hoy Mountain, Ladore School, Swallow Canyon

Diamond Breaks gets its name from the breaks in Diamond Mountain carved by Hoy, Chokecherry, Davis and other creeks as they drain into the Green River. Local tradition has it that Diamond Mountain itself was named after

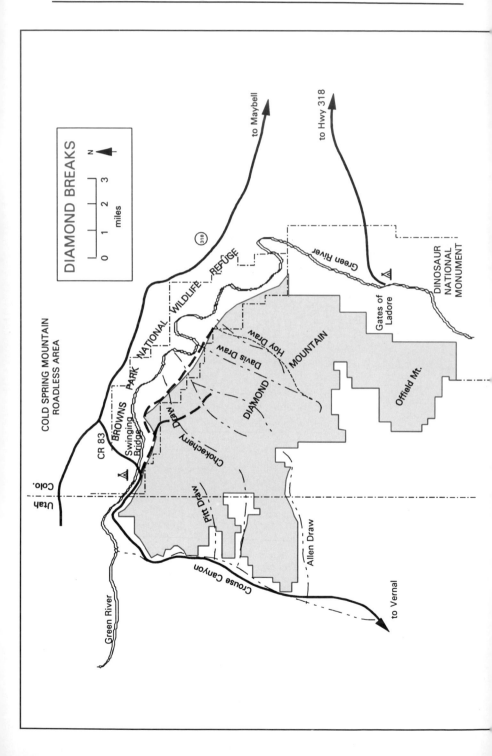

DIAMOND BREAKS

N

0 1 2 3
miles

the exploits of a shyster in the late 1800s who salted diamonds on the mountain and lured unsuspecting Eastern investors into parting with their money in a get-rich-quick diamond mining scheme. Of course, the shyster departed the region soon after, with money in hand and nary a diamond to be found in the barren geology of "Diamond Mountain."

Diamond Breaks is distinctive for its variety of topography and vegetation. Piñon-juniper–covered ridges and peaks rise to 8,700 feet, a startling contrast to the gentle sagebrush-covered plain found in Browns Park. The rugged mountains of Diamond Breaks are broken by open draws and stands of aspen, providing a complement to the mighty Canyon of Ladore on the Green River in adjacent Dinosaur National Monument. The semiarid, dissected mountains of Diamond Breaks extend the canyon ecosystems of Dinosaur National Monument; together they offer a recreational range from whitewater boating deep within Dinosaur's canyons to rock climbing and ridge hiking high above in Diamond Breaks.

The ridges and peaks of Diamond Breaks offer spectacular panoramic views of features in Utah, Colorado and Wyoming: the Green River plain, the mighty Canyon of Ladore, gentle Cold Springs Mountain and the snow-capped peaks of the Uintas, the Flat Tops and the Zirkel Range. A majestic, gnarled ponderosa pine forest covers the southern edge of the area, growing out of bare rock in many places. Open draws and hillsides create a rainbow of color in early spring as flowers of every conceivable hue burst forth among the sagebrush.

Diamond Breaks has a high potential for significant archaeological finds. Granaries, petroglyphs and widespread lithic scatter dating to the Fremont era have been recorded in the area. There are rumors of wickiups as well.

The area is also rich in wildlife, including mule deer, elk, black bear and mountain lion. Diamond Breaks provides critical deer winter range and encompasses a major portion of the range for a herd of 250 to 300 elk. Pronghorn roam the lower valleys near the wildlife refuge.

Several good hikes exist along the northern edge of Diamond Breaks up the creeks that create the breaks. Beginning at the Swinging Bridge across the Green River in the far western reaches of Browns Park National Wildlife Refuge (Moffat County Road 83), follow the four-wheel-drive track east along the south bank of the river. This track skirts the edge of the BLM roadless area and ultimately leads to the western half of the Gates of Ladore within the National Monument. The first major tributary reached along this track is Chokecherry Draw. An abandoned four-wheel-drive trail leads a couple of short miles up Chokecherry Draw to a long-forgotten homestead. The homestead includes the foundations of several structures, a cool spring, wild roses and fruit trees gone wild, all in a setting of lush greenery amid a desert forest of piñon-juniper.

Hoy Draw is the easternmost tributary in Diamond Breaks. Hoy Draw intersects the four-wheel-drive track about eight miles from the Swinging Bridge. An old trail can be followed several miles up Hoy Draw to Hoy Spring, where a cold, clear stream of water pours out of a small opening in the hillside. Shortly past the spring, the drainage reaches a low saddle, beyond which are the headwaters of Davis Draw. Davis Draw is a broad valley that can be followed south to private land marking the southern boundary of the Diamond Breaks roadless area. Alternatively, hikers can turn north and bushwhack through thick brush back to Browns Park and end up a mile west of where they started up Hoy Draw.

There is excellent access to the western boundary of Diamond Breaks from the Crouse Canyon road in Utah. From the Swinging Bridge, Moffat County Road 83 heads west into Utah and soon enters the rugged and narrow confines of Crouse Canyon. The road breaks out of Crouse Canyon after several miles, and a major drainage, Pitt Draw, enters from the east. A four-wheel-drive trail provides the route for a hike up the short length of Pitt Draw.

Approximately three miles south of Pitt Draw, an unnamed drainage intersects Crouse Creek. This 3.5-mile-long drainage consists of lush, flower-covered meadows and dense thickets, surrounded with ridges capped by rock outcrops that afford unrestricted views of the three-state region. Douglas-fir and aspen hug the north slopes of the ridges and create unexpected forest glens. Again, an old vehicle track provides the easiest hiking route along the valley bottom and ultimately leads to a short scramble to a saddle affording views of Cold Springs Mountain and other area features.

The Crouse Canyon road ultimately leads to Vernal, Utah. To get there from Vernal, follow the signs to Diamond Mountain that depart from Highway 191 a couple of blocks north of the center of town.

Sawmill Canyon, Dave Cooper

30 DINOSAUR NATIONAL MONUMENT ADJACENT AREAS

Location:	North boundary of Dinosaur National Monument, 25 miles northwest of the town of Dinosaur
Elevation Range:	5,800 – 8,000 feet
Vegetation/Ecosystem:	Ponderosa pine; piñon-juniper; sagebrush
Roadless Acreage:	31,340 acres
Wilderness Status:	Not proposed for wilderness by BLM
Special Features:	Views into Dinosaur; access to Yampa River canyon
USGS Maps:	Canyon of Ladore South, Greystone, Jones Hole, Indian Water Canyon, Limestone Hill, Lone Mountain (15'), Zenobia Peak

Six roadless areas are contiguous to the north boundary of Dinosaur National Monument, extending the entire length of the boundary. The eastern five areas

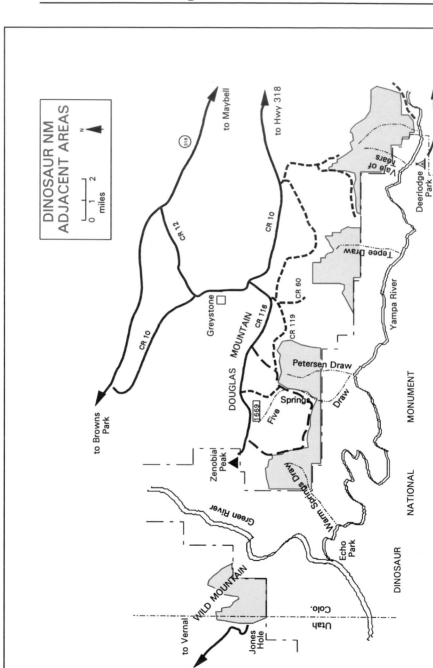

DINOSAUR NM
ADJACENT AREAS

N

0 1 2
miles

to Maybell

to Hwy 318

to Hwy 40

Vale of
Tears

Deerlodge
Park

CR 12

CR 10

Tepee Draw

Yampa River

Greystone

CR 118

CR 60

DOUGLAS MOUNTAIN

CR 119

CR 10

Petersen Draw

to Browns
Park

1669

Springs

Draw

Five

MONUMENT

Zenobial Peak

Warm Springs Draw

Green River

NATIONAL

Echo
Park

DINOSAUR

WILD MOUNTAIN

to Vernal

Colo.

Utah

Jones
Hole

together encompass the southern slopes and drainages of Douglas Mountain. Rolling ridges covered by piñon-juniper forest, broken by sagebrush and grass parks, are typical of the areas. Deer, elk and mountain lion inhabit the areas. Peregrine falcons, which nest nearby in the cliffs of the Yampa River Canyon, use the areas for hunting. Wild Mountain is the sixth area, west of the Canyon of Ladore along the Colorado-Utah state line.

The largest of the six is Vale of Tears at the Monument's extreme eastern end, directly across from the Deerlodge Park campground and boat launch on the Yampa River. The Vale of Tears is an extremely scenic drainage of red, yellow, tan and brown badlands near its confluence with the Yampa River. At its higher elevations, piñon-juniper appear as well as ponderosa pine. Vale of Tears is reached either by one of several very rough four-wheel-drive roads from the top of Douglas Mountain or more easily from the valleys of the Yampa and Little Snake rivers. Take County Road 125 north from the National Park Service Deerlodge Park access road approximately three miles. At this point, a road turns west and crosses the Little Snake River. Once across the Little Snake, the road winds its way south to the Yampa River. The road terminates at the mouth of the Vale of Tears, which makes a fine starting point for hikes, as do any of several four-wheel-drive trails that branch off before then. Sawmill Canyon, east of Vale of Tears, may be followed six or seven miles to Allred Peak, the highest point in the area.

Ant Hills, Chew Winter Camp and Petersen Draw are in truth one contiguous roadless area. Mapping errors by BLM during its wilderness inventory in 1980 resulted in the current distinction, but there are no vehicle routes of any kind in Big Joe Draw and Warm Springs Draw. The three areas are nestled in the L on the remote north side of Dinosaur National Monument. Along with the Tepee Draw roadless area to their east, the areas share almost 20 miles of boundary with Dinosaur National Monument. All of the areas are reached via the Douglas Mountain road, Moffat County Road 116, which ultimately terminates at the Zenobia Peak fire lookout. Follow state Highway 318 west from Maybell to County Road 12 (the turnoff to Greystone) and head south from Greystone several miles up onto Douglas Mountain on CR 116. Douglas Mountain is covered with stands of stately ponderosa pine. The roadless areas generally begin in the fringes of this pine forest and descend south into the desert tributary canyons of the Yampa River.

The boundary of the Petersen Draw roadless area is reached via County Road 119, which departs from CR 116 soon after gaining the crest of Douglas Mountain. Either Petersen Draw or Buck Draw may be followed five or six miles to the Yampa River.

Ant Hills and Chew Winter Camp are reached from BLM road 1669, which heads down Five Springs Draw from CR 116 about eight miles across Douglas Mountain. The road deteriorates into a four-wheel-drive trail that parallels the monument boundary west to Big Joe Draw. The road and draw define the boundaries of Ant Hills and Chew Winter Camp roadless areas. Five Springs Draw is the eastern boundary of Chew Winter Camp, and a three-mile hike down it takes you to the Yampa River. The major feature in Ant Hills is the upper few miles of Warm Springs Draw. Following Warm Springs Draw downstream takes you to the rapid and river campsite of the same name on the Yampa River inside the Monument.

Tepee Draw roadless area is reached from one of several rough four-wheel-drive trails that branch off of County Roads 60 and 119 south of the mountain crest. One four-wheel-drive trail leaves CR 60 and winds across the east portion of Douglas Mountain to the top of Tepee Draw and Corral Springs Draw. A several-mile hike takes you down Tepee Draw to the Yampa River and Tepee Rapid.

Wild Mountain, the westernmost roadless area, lies astride the Colorado-Utah state line on the northwest boundary of the Monument. Wild Mountain is a prominent landmark, dominating the view from the Echo Park and Harpers Corner overlooks within Dinosaur National Monument and forming the steep, northern backdrop to Jones Hole. The access to Wild Mountain is from Vernal, Utah. Take Highway 191 north and turn right a couple of blocks from the town center at the sign to Diamond Mountain and Jones Hole. Take the Diamond Mountain road to the Jones Hole National Fish Hatchery, following the signs to Jones Hole all the way. Just before dropping down into the valley and the fish hatchery, an old four-wheel-drive trail branches off to the north. This trail leads steeply to the top of Wild Mountain. Wild Mountain affords spectacular views of the Canyon of Ladore, the Yampa Canyon and the Uinta Mountains.

Dave Cooper

31   OIL SPRING MOUNTAIN

Location:	25 miles south of Rangely
Elevation Range:	6,000 – 8,550 feet
Vegetation/Ecosystem:	Sagebrush; piñon-juniper; Douglas-fir; mountain-mahogany–oakbrush
Roadless Acreage:	17,740 acres
Wilderness Status:	Not proposed for wilderness by BLM
Special Features:	Wildlife habitat; petroglyphs
USGS Maps:	Big Foundation Creek, East Evacuation Creek, Texas Creek, Texas Mountain

Oil Spring Mountain, an isolated remnant of wild country in the oil and gas country around Rangely in far western Colorado, has been described as an oasis in a sea of development. Because this forested mesa has thus far escaped extensive development, it is an important haven for wildlife herds north of Douglas Pass.

The northern slopes of Oil Spring Mountain rise through dense conifer forest to small stands of aspen shaded beneath sandstone cliffs. On southern

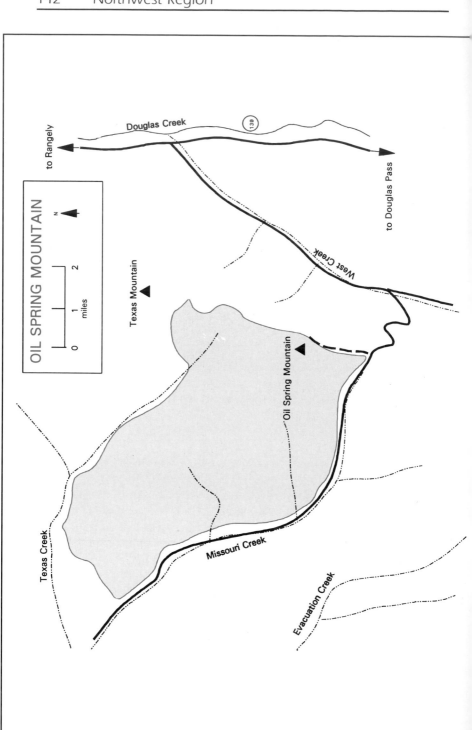

exposures, mountain-mahogany, oakbrush, piñon and juniper prevail. The numerous vegetation types result in utilization of the area by a diversity of wildlife. Oil Spring Mountain is a black bear concentration area, unique for lands in the lower White River drainage in western Colorado. An important mule deer migration route is located on the northeast side of Oil Spring Mountain. Mule deer summer on the upper slopes of the mountain and use the lower elevations for winter range. Elk use the upper elevations on a year-round basis, and an elk winter concentration area is located around Red Cedar Spring. Mountain lions are also frequent in the area.

State Highway 139, the Douglas Pass road from Grand Junction to Rangely, provides access to Oil Spring Mountain. Oil Spring Mountain is approached via the road in West Creek, which branches west from the highway approximately 11 miles north of Douglas Pass. After several miles, a road forks right from West Creek and climbs in a switchback to a low pass. This saddle marks the southeast corner of the roadless area, and several grassy meadows provide pleasant camping spots along here. From the saddle, a hiker can bushwhack through dense brush up the ridge to the highest point of the mountain, though the mountain top is heavily forested also, and the best vantage points are obtained by maneuvering to one of the rims of the summit plateau.

Continuing over the pass, the road drops into Missouri Creek and veers northwest, forming the western boundary of the roadless area. Several tributary canyons in the lower segments of the drainage offer routes into the roadless area. Cultural sites including artifacts and petroglyph panels are most common in this portion of the area where several alcoves are carved into sandstone cliffs. Dating of artifacts indicates the area was occupied from approximately 7,000 years ago to the late 1870s.

University of Colorado Wilderness Study Group

32   PIÑON RIDGE

Location:	30 miles northwest of Meeker
Elevation Range:	5,600 – 7,400 feet
Vegetation/Ecosystem:	Piñon-juniper; sagebrush
Roadless Acreage:	20,100 acres
Wilderness Status:	Not proposed for wilderness by BLM
Special Features:	Scenic vistas; White River frontage
USGS Maps:	Elk Springs (15'), Rough Gulch, Smizer Gulch

Piñon Ridge consists of rolling hills immediately north of the White River. These hills overlook a broad basin of high mesas and deep arroyos from a sheer and abrupt bluff. Sweeping scenic vistas of the White River valley, the Danforth Hills and the mesas of the Rangely Basin are obtained from Piñon Ridge. Piñon Ridge is one of the very few undeveloped areas of the lower White River drainage.

Piñon Ridge is an arid area, cut by numerous seasonal streams that create a spiderweb of isolated drainages. Sagebrush, grasses and cacti cover the lower

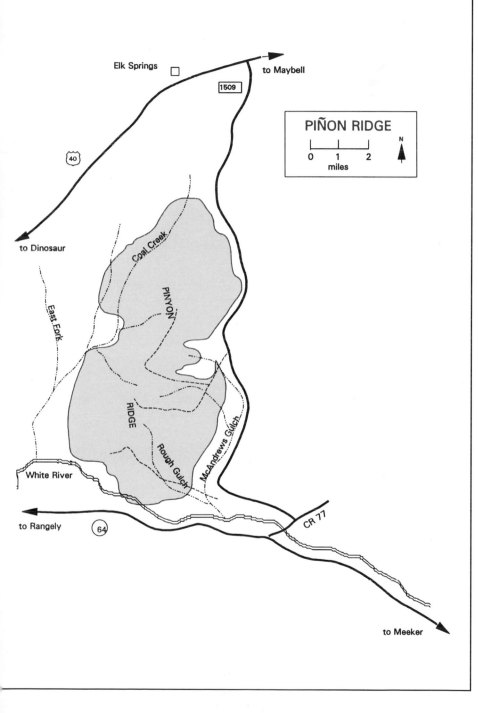

elevations, and piñon-juniper forest blankets the hills and ridges. A wide variety of wildlife exists within the area, including eagles and other raptors that build nests along ridge outcrops and prey on extensive prairie dog populations. Larger mammals such as deer, coyotes and mountain lions inhabit the forested slopes.

Piñon Ridge is particularly suited for hiking, owing to its outstanding scenic qualities and the presence of overgrown four-wheel-drive trails that provide excellent foot and horse trails for exploration. Steep canyons and mesas in the western sections of Piñon Ridge offer challenging hikes and climbs for the more adventurous. Piñon Ridge is most easily reached via a new road recently constructed by BLM. The road generally forms the eastern boundary of the roadless area and connects highways 40 and 64.

From Highway 40, turn south on BLM road 1509 about 4 miles east of Elk Springs. The road heads south along the east side of Piñon Ridge and eventually connects with Rio Blanco County Road 77. County Road 77 leads directly to Highway 64 across the White River. All of these roads may require four-wheel-drive vehicles in inclement weather. Any of several overgrown four-wheel-drive trails lead into Piñon Ridge from road 1509.

Mark Pearson

33   VERMILLION BASIN

Location:	80 miles west of Craig, 20 miles north of Dinosaur National Monument
Elevation Range:	5,700 – 8,120 feet
Vegetation/Ecosystem:	Piñon-juniper forest; saltbush desert
Roadless Acreage:	88,340 acres
Wilderness Status:	Not proposed for wilderness by BLM
Special Features:	Colorful badlands; petroglyphs; spectacular vistas; rare plants
USGS Maps:	Coffee Pot Spring, G Spring, Hawatha, Irish Canyon, Sheepherder Springs, Vermillion Mesa

Vermillion Basin consists of vividly colored badlands and is host to a large number of very rare plants and plant communities. It includes all or parts of five areas identified by the Colorado Natural Areas Program as potential Research Natural Areas for protection of rare plants. In addition, an array of geologic formations, petroglyphs, seashell fossil beds, soft-rock canyons and

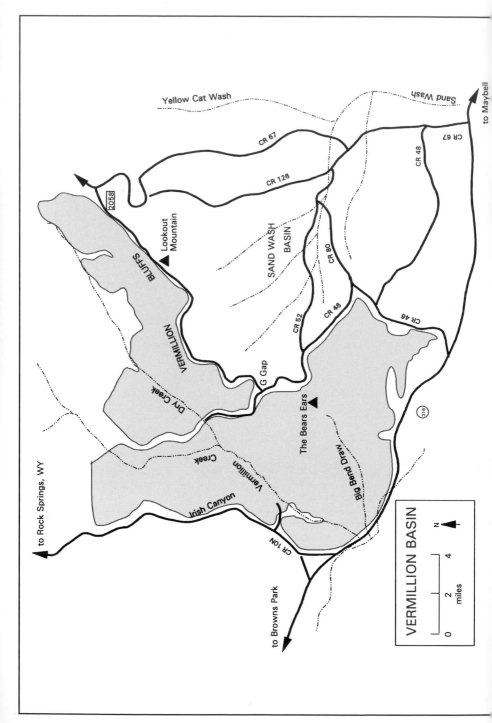

VERMILLION BASIN

varying topography make this area a delight for hikers.

The central Vermillion Basin, including the Dry Creek area, is a stunning desert canyon, with a few sandstone layers shaping, coloring and breaking the soft sediments. Standing on one peninsula of the plateau, with a rich green canyon bottom lying below, one has the sensation of standing next to a small Grand Canyon. All around lie beautiful and delicate badlands.

Vermillion Canyon contains one of the most spectacular collections of petroglyphs found in Colorado. At least eight panels, four of them with dozens of petroglyphs, line the canyon walls. One petroglyph rises over six feet high on a ledge 40 feet above the canyon floor. Other petroglyphs feature bow hunting, religious figures, coyotes, elk, deer and footprints. The canyon itself is similarly spectacular, with desert varnish, sculpted sandstone and a steep crumbling cliff rising more than 1,000 feet.

The mouth of Vermillion Canyon is reached via Highway 318 and Moffat County Road 10N. Approximately three miles north on 10N a road branches east. Follow this road a mile or so until you reach a two-track road that veers north toward the base of the uplifted ridge; (the main road descends a steep hill to a ranch on private land). After parking your vehicle, find a route down the steep canyon slopes to the bottom of Vermillion Creek and follow the canyon upstream. The canyon itself is relatively short, consisting of only a couple of miles of stream meanders incised into the uplifted ridge. Beyond this ridge, the stream course breaks out into an open, shallow basin defined by brilliantly colored badlands.

Another hike begins atop Lookout Mountain in the northeastern section of the area. Lookout Mountain is reached most easily via a network of county roads, beginning with the Sand Wash Road (CR 67) that leaves Highway 318 a couple of miles past the Little Snake River bridge. Follow CR 67 approximately 25 miles north to BLM road 2058 and turn southwest for several miles to Lookout Mountain. From Lookout Mountain, the adjacent Vermillion Bluffs create a dramatic escarpment rising more than 1,700 feet from the creek below. Hikers can pick a route down the colorful badlands, earth flows and slumps along a ridge or an abandoned four-wheel-drive trail. For plant lovers, Lookout Mountain contains four plant taxa listed by the Colorado Natural Areas Program as of state concern, including the only known occurrences in Colorado of the hairy townsendia and the capitate chicken sate.

A third access takes hikers into the middle of the Vermillion Basin roadless area. Again leaving Highway 318 at the Sand Wash Road, take County Road 48 west approximately five miles north of the highway and follow it and County Roads 46 and 52 — 20 miles or more west to G Gap. G Gap Research Natural Area includes two plant associations of state concern and the best condition of occurrence of the regional endemic plant, *Cymopterus duchesnensis* (Duchesne biscuitroot). From G Gap, descend west to Dry Creek. The road crosses Dry Creek at this point and cuts the roadless area into two units. Several hikes are possible upstream and downstream from here, following abandoned four-wheel-drive trails, cattle trails or the creek bed. Upstream, hikers skirt the base of the Vermillion Bluffs; downstream lies a broad valley flanked by jagged spires of assorted fantastic shapes and colors.

Mark Pearson

34   YAMPA RIVER

Location:	15 miles southwest of Craig
Elevation Range:	6,200–7,000 feet
Vegetation/Ecosystem:	Piñon-juniper; cottonwood riparian zone
Roadless Acreage:	15,960 acres
Wilderness Status:	Not proposed for wilderness by BLM
Special Features:	10 miles of Yampa River; big-game herds; raptors
USGS Maps:	Axial, Horse Gulch, Round Bottom

The Yampa River is usually considered the least impacted of Colorado's mighty rivers. Downstream portions of the river are protected within Dinosaur National Monument, and the river's headwaters are protected within the Flat Tops Wilderness. Yet a third sample of the Yampa ecosystem — described here — can be found in a segment of the river midway along its course through the rangelands of northwest Colorado.

The Yampa River roadless area includes the stretch of the Yampa west of

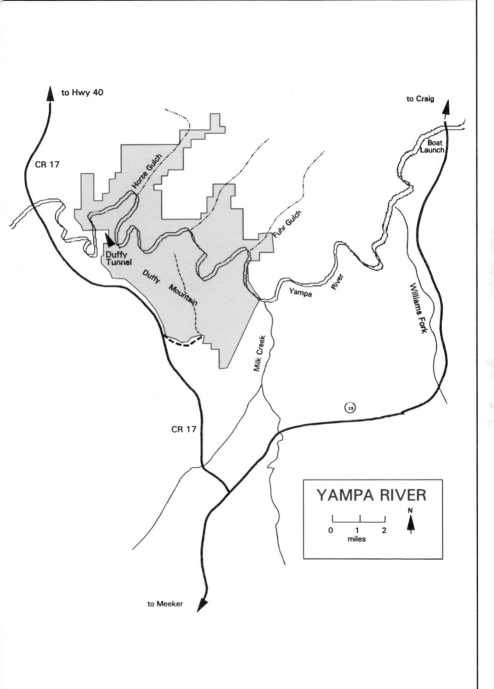

to Hwy 40

to Craig

Boat
Launch

CR 17

Horse Gulch

Duffy
Tunnel

Duffy Mountain

Fuhr Gulch

Yampa River

Williams Fork

Milk Creek

13

CR 17

YAMPA RIVER

0   1   2
miles

N

to Meeker

Milk Creek where the river slices through Duffy Mountain. The main body of the area is managed by BLM as the Little Yampa/Juniper Canyon Special Recreation Management Area (SRMA) for recreational rafting, canoeing, camping and hunting. As an SRMA, the area receives more frequent patrolling, special management for protecting its visual qualities and additional consideration for public access. Visitors will likely see extensive evidence of the large numbers of deer and elk that winter in the area.

The roadless area encompasses more than 10 miles of the Yampa River and includes a portion of the river that would be inundated by the Juniper Mountain dam proposed by the Colorado River Water Conservation District. The dam proposal is largely defunct owing to the negative impact construction would have on the several endangered species of fish in the river, including the Colorado River squawfish and the humpback chub, and to the poor economics surrounding the project. The river district is still pursuing studies of the proposed dam, however.

River travel is a popular means of discovering the wilderness values of the area. A serene riparian ecosystem lines the river banks; the cottonwoods that populate several large parks offer inviting campsites to boaters. The launch point for canoe or raft trips is a boat ramp and parking area at the Highway 13 bridge across the Yampa several miles south of Craig. The river cuts wide meanders through private land for the first few miles and then enters public land a mile below the Williams Fork confluence. There are scattered tracts of private land along the river for the next 25 miles until the Yampa exits Duffy Mountain into irrigated pastures (the roadless area begins approximately 10 miles downriver at the Milk Creek confluence).

Canoeists should leave the river at the highway bridges at Moffat County Roads 17 and 53 to avoid the significant rapids downstream in Juniper Canyon.

Hiking access to Duffy Mountain is gained via County Road 17. This road connects Highways 40 and 13, approximately 19 miles west of Craig on Highway 40, or 26 miles south of Craig on Highway 13. From County Road 17, BLM Road 1596 heads east toward Duffy Mountain south of the river. From atop Duffy Mountain, a visitor has views northeast to Craig and west toward Juniper Canyon. Duffy Mountain and the other ridges and valleys surrounding the Yampa River are gently rolling, sage-covered hills and provide innumerable opportunities for adventurous route-finding.

Canoeing through Little Yampa Canyon, Yampa River. Mark Pearson photograph.

CENTRAL COLORADO

Opposite: Limestone cliffs high above Deep Creek. John Fielder photograph.

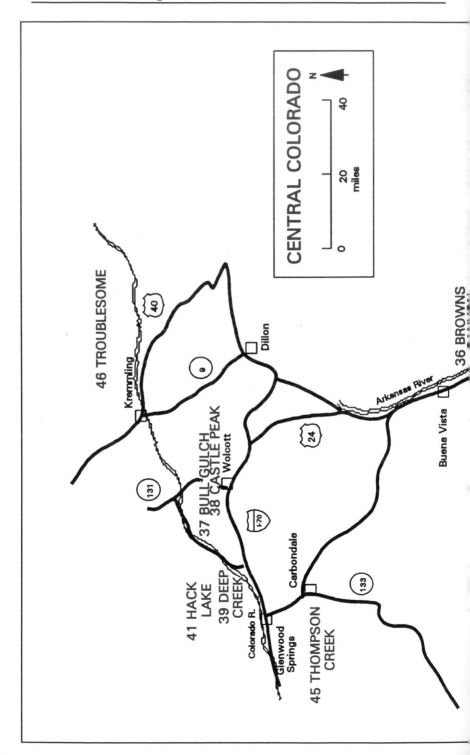

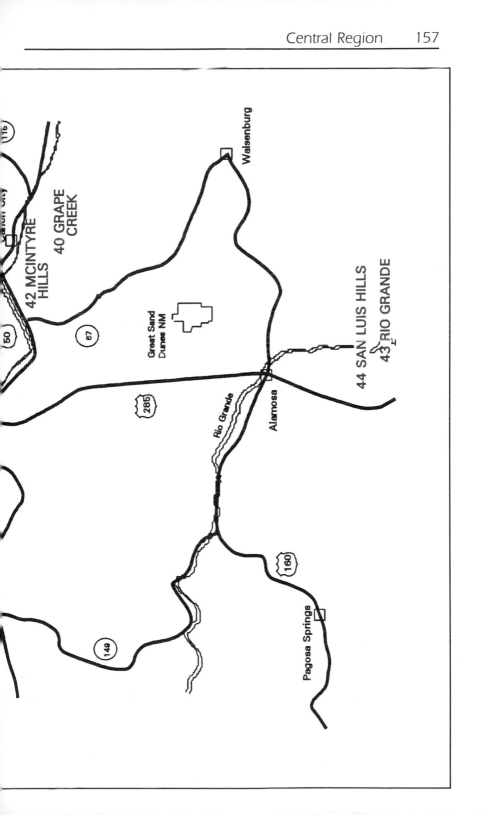

35   BEAVER CREEK

Location:	23 miles northeast of Canon City
Elevation Range:	6,000 – 10,000 feet
Vegetation/Ecosystem:	Piñon-juniper; ponderosa pine; Douglas-fir; aspen
Roadless Acreage:	26,150 acres
Wilderness Status:	20,750 acres proposed for wilderness by BLM
Special Features:	Trout fishery; granite canyons; bighorn sheep
USGS Maps:	Big Bull Mountain, Mt. Big Chief, Mt. Pittsburg, Phantom Canyon

Beaver Creek is composed of extremely scenic and rugged terrain on the dramatic south slope of the Pikes Peak massif. The canyons and tributaries of Beaver Creek, which form the heart of the area, are deeply sculpted in granite reminiscent of the spectacular sandstone canyons of the Colorado Plateau and are highlighted by groves of ponderosa pine. Beaver Creek is a sizable stream year round, and its headwaters are at the top of Pikes Peak.

In the Beaver Creek area, life zones range from the upper Sonoran to the montane, from desert species of plants to verdant pine-spruce-fir forests and meadows. Beaver Creek is a renowned cold-water fishery, featuring a variety of trout, including cutthroat. One of the highlights of any trip through Beaver Creek is a sighting of one of the 50 or so bighorn sheep that are residents of the area. Other terrestrial animals include mule deer, occasional elk, numerous black bear, mountain lion, golden eagles and, of course, beaver. Endangered peregrine falcons have also been sighted.

The Colorado Division of Wildlife owns and manages 870 acres of the streambeds of East and West Beaver creeks and the main stem for several miles below their confluence. A cooperative management agreement currently exists between the Division and the BLM that ensures that this critical inholding is managed to retain wilderness values.

Several trails depart from Division of Wildlife lands at the mouth of Beaver Creek Canyon. The trail head at Beaver Creek State Wildlife Area is reached from either U.S. Highway 50 between Pueblo and Canon City or state Highway 115 south of Colorado Springs. From Highway 50, turn north on the Phantom Canyon road (state Highway 67), drive several miles, turn east on County Road 123, and then turn onto County Road 132. From Highway 115, drive directly to County Road 123 at the curve north of Penrose and then to County Road 132. Hikers can leave their vehicles at the corral parking area that is

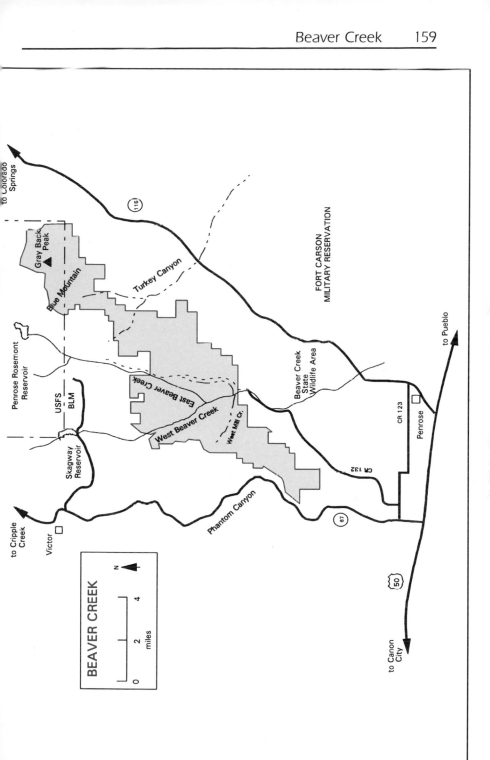

BEAVER CREEK

N

0   2   4
miles

about one mile past the bridge at the wildlife area. There is camping at the wildlife area (no facilities) or at a private campground at Indian Springs in Phantom Canyon, approximately 25 minutes' drive from the wildlife area.

A well-maintained trail heads north up Beaver Creek from the parking area. The trail climbs the hillside and generally parallels the course of the streambed several hundred feet uphill to the confluence of East and West Beaver creeks, three miles from the parking lot. It is also possible to follow the creek itself,

Looking down the West Fork of Beaver Creek, Beaver Creek Wilderness Study Area. John Fielder photograph.

though this requires several stream crossings and some bushwhacking. Keep a sharp eye out for poison ivy and rattlesnakes in addition to bighorn sheep.

A second trail branches right from the first at Trail Gulch and winds its way approximately five miles north across rugged country, where it connects with East Beaver Creek. Hikers can loop back to their start by bushwhacking along East Beaver Creek downstream to the confluence, and thence following the Beaver Creek trail to the wildlife area. A shorter loop also is possible. Follow Trail Gulch upstream to a signed left turn that leads over a ridge to the confluence of East and West Beaver Creeks. Above the confluence, the stream becomes particularly wild with cascades, small waterfalls and narrowing canyon walls.

Other tributaries without trails, such as West Mill Creek, are available for exploration by those in search of undisturbed solitude. Consult the topographic maps to determine suitable routes into any of the canyons that branch off of Beaver Creek and Trail Gulch.

John Fielder

36   BROWNS CANYON

Location:	Six miles southeast of Buena Vista
Elevation Range:	7,500 – 10,000 feet
Vegetation/Ecosystem:	Piñon-juniper; cottonwood; ponderosa pine; aspen
Roadless Acreage:	21,350 acres (includes 14,720 acres of Forest Service land)
Wilderness Status:	6,614 acres proposed for wilderness by BLM
Special Features:	Arkansas River; rugged isolation; scenic vistas
USGS Maps:	Antero Reservoir (15'), Buena Vista (15'), Cameron Mountain (15'), Poncha Springs (15')

Browns Canyon of the Arkansas River is widely known among whitewater boating enthusiasts. The busiest stretch of the river, Browns Canyon totals 85,000 visitor user days annually, according to figures compiled by BLM.

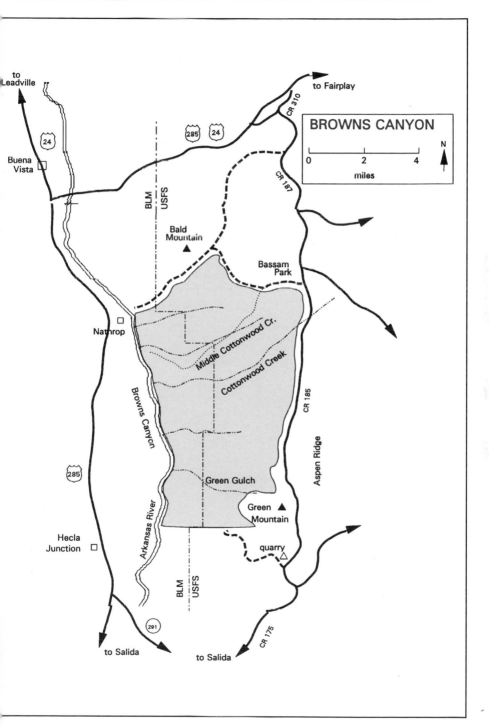

to Leadville

to Fairplay

CR 310

BROWNS CANYON

N

0   2   4
miles

24

285 24

Buena
Vista

BLM
USFS

CR 187

Bald
Mountain ▲

Bassam
Park

Nathrop

Middle Cottonwood Cr.

Cottonwood Creek

CR 185

Browns Canyon

Aspen Ridge

285

Green Gulch

Green ▲
Mountain

Hecla
Junction

Arkansas River

quarry △

BLM
USFS

291

CR 175

to Salida

to Salida

to Salida

However, the majority of these visitors never set foot within the rugged and isolated slopes and gulches that climb steeply east of the river and culminate in Aspen Ridge, approximately five miles from the river.

The Browns Canyon roadless area consists of both BLM land adjacent to the Arkansas River and portions of the San Isabel National Forest. The BLM lands nearer to the river are characterized by rocky, broken slopes dissected by a half-dozen rugged drainages. Forests of piñon pine and juniper gradually give way to stands of ponderosa pine and, finally, aspen as you crest the ridge. Rocky outcrops throughout the area provide expansive views of the Collegiate Range. Many species of wildlife prize the area's isolation, and more than 100 bighorn sheep call the area home. This block of land is without marked trails, and the forbidding topography dissuades many potential visitors from venturing deep within it.

Hiking choices include skirting along high ridges and obtaining bird's-eye views of the Collegiates or trekking down tributaries to the river's edge. Chaffee County Road 185 parallels the higher, eastern boundary of the area and is the most direct access for hikes. From Salida, follow Chaffee County 175 to County Road 185, which is a passable though occasionally rough two-wheel-drive route. From the north, turn on County Road 310 from U.S. Highways 24 and 285 and then follow County Road 187 to 185.

Middle Cottonwood Creek is a substantial stream that offers one of the best routes to the river. The route follows a four-wheel-drive trail where it leaves County Road 185 in Bassam Park and soon heads down the streambed of Middle Cottonwood, reaching the river in about seven miles. An even wilder route to the river is obtained via the main Cottonwood Creek. Again park along County Road 185, at one of the branches of the stream in Bassam Park or Coons Park, and follow the creekbed five or six miles cross-country to the Arkansas. Return the same way or climb uphill along one of the many rocky ridges back over the crest of Aspen Ridge to your starting point.

A short hike across meadows and through groves of aspen and ponderosa takes hikers to the crest of Aspen Ridge at the south end of the area. Follow County Road 185 to the watershed divide at the top of Green Gulch, and then strike out cross-country along the fenceline toward the ridge less than a mile to the west. From the ridge, the intrepid can drop down Sawmill Gulch or Green Gulch to the river.

The Bald Mountain Road forms the northern boundary of the area and provides access to Little Cottonwood Creek. Bald Mountain Road leaves County Road 187 a mile or two south of Highways 24 and 285 and drops down the slope to the river near Ruby Mountain.

John Fielder

37   BULL GULCH

Location:	13 miles north of Eagle
Elevation Range:	6,400 –9,700 feet
Vegetation/Ecosystem:	Piñon-juniper; sagebrush; Douglas-fir; aspen; spruce-fir
Roadless Acreage:	15,004 acres
Wilderness Status:	10,415 acres proposed for wilderness by BLM
Special Features:	Colorado River; colorful geology; scenic vistas
USGS Maps:	Burns South, Gypsum

Bull Gulch is one of the few roadless areas along the mid-elevation reaches of the Colorado River. Bull Gulch creates a scenic carved basin amid the forested red-rock country of the Colorado River drainage above the Eagle River confluence. It encompasses a remarkable ecological transition point between the alpine birthplace of the Colorado and the famous desert canyon country through which the river travels on its way to the sea.

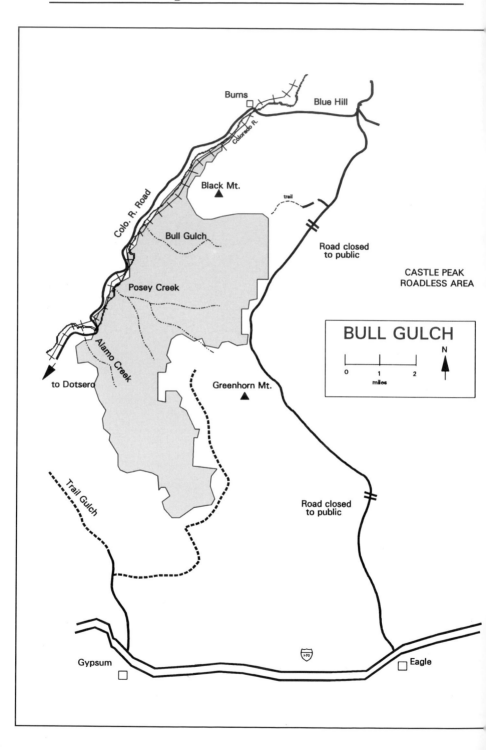

Burns

Blue Hill

Colorado R.

Black Mt. ▲

Colo. R. Road

trail

Road closed
to public

Bull Gulch

CASTLE PEAK
ROADLESS AREA

Posey Creek

BULL GULCH

Alamo Creek

to Dotsero

0   1   2
miles

N ▲

Greenhorn Mt. ▲

Road closed
to public

Trail Gulch

I-70

Gypsum

Eagle

Dropping precipitously from a forested rim at 9,700 feet, Bull Gulch has eroded the deep red formations of Maroon Bells fame as it drains into the Colorado River. The entrance to Bull Gulch is a labyrinth of twisting corridors and sculpted bowls carved through maroon sandstone. The roar of the river is immediately left behind, to be replaced by the silence of the canyon, broken only by the sound of dripping seeps that line the canyon walls.

The lower reaches of Bull Gulch are covered by dense piñon-juniper forests. These give way at higher elevations to stands of aspen, Douglas-fir, blue spruce and ponderosa pine. Bull Gulch is a bouquet of color in the fall owing to brilliant golden aspen that highlight an already spectacular blend of vivid red sandstone, dark green spruce and fir, and majestic blue sky, all capped by towering cliffs of blinding white sandstone.

Bull Gulch provides important deer and elk winter range and supports predator populations of mountain lion, bobcat and coyote. Prairie falcons nest here, and hunting perches for endangered bald eagles have been identified as well.

The best overland access to Bull Gulch is via the Eby Creek road which parallels the eastern rim of Bull Gulch. This road connects I-70 at Eagle with the Colorado River near Burns, but the road is closed to the public from the south end about four miles from the Eagle exit on I-70.

Instead, hikers should travel the Colorado River road from McCoy or Dotsero to the summit of Blue Hill, about three miles east of Burns. Turn south onto the western-most of the two dirt roads at this intersection and follow the road about 3.5 to a four-wheel-drive trail that heads west toward Black Mountain. (The main road is closed at a gate another half-mile down the road.) This four-wheel-drive trail ends in a mile or so and offers good access along game trails into the headwaters of Bull Gulch. Several good primitive camping sites exist along this trail amid scattered stands of ponderosa pine. The Bull Gulch basin consists of open, sagebrush-covered hillsides ringed by aspen and spruce-fir forests below the basin rim.

There are several other overland routes into the rugged south end of the roadless area around Alamo Creek and Posey Creek. From the Colorado River road about 13 miles north of Dotsero, an old road heads up Alamo Creek for a mile or two and then fades to a rough trail.

Access to Posey Creek requires a significant amount of travel along a network of four-wheel-drive trails in the Greenhorn Mountain area. From the Gypsum exit on I-70, head north up Road Gulch five or six miles and turn east onto a four-wheel-drive trail that ultimately winds east and north about 12 miles to Big Red Hill. The road ends at private land, but a trail offers a route around the private land and into Posey Creek. It is likely that few other visitors will be encountered owing to the physical obstacles of this access route.

The mouth of Bull Gulch is best approached via the Colorado River. From the river, Bull Gulch has incised a short slickrock canyon that opens in the wide basin described above. A short loop hike of five or six miles is possible by climbing out of Bull Gulch north into the adjacent unnamed drainage and returning down it to the river, and thence to Bull Gulch.

The Colorado River along this stretch includes several Class II rapids and a couple of bridge pilings that are serious river hazards. The nearest river launch sites above Bull Gulch are at the BLM's Pinball Recreation Site (about 1.5 miles upstream of Bull Gulch) or at Burns. Pinball Rapid can pose a hazard because of a railroad bridge just below Bull Gulch. At Twin Bridges (another bridge hazard) or Cottonwood Island, about three miles below Bull Gulch, there are informal takeout sites that may require obtaining permission from private landowners.

Developed recreation sites with boat takeouts are at Lions Gulch (12 river miles downstream) and at Sheep Gulch (five miles farther downstream from Lions Gulch.) Jacks Flat offers a good campsite a couple of miles below Bull Gulch on river left for boaters wishing to make an overnight trip.

The BLM has published a river map for the Colorado River between Kremmling and Dotsero. Anyone wishing to float the river segment along Bull Gulch should contact the BLM office in Kremmling or Glenwood Springs for a copy of this map.

John Fielder

38   CASTLE PEAK

Location:	Eight miles north of Eagle
Elevation Range:	8,400 – 11,275 feet
Vegetation/Ecosystem:	Sagebrush; oakbrush; spruce-fir; aspen
Roadless Acreage:	16,180 acres
Wilderness Status:	Not proposed for wilderness by BLM
Special Features:	Craggy Castle Peak; scenic vistas; dense forest
USGS Maps:	Castle Peak, Eagle

Castle Peak is a distinctive, and aptly named, promontory readily apparent from I-70 between Wolcott and Eagle. The roadless area spans mid-level elevations from 8,000 to 11,000 feet, generally below the level of most designated Forest Service wilderness areas and well above the more typical desert canyon and plateau lands of the BLM. Castle Peak supports a wide range of plant and animal habitat, from mixed sage and grasslands on its extreme east side, through meadow-like openings intermixed with aspen groves, to spruce-fir forests with trees of substantial size.

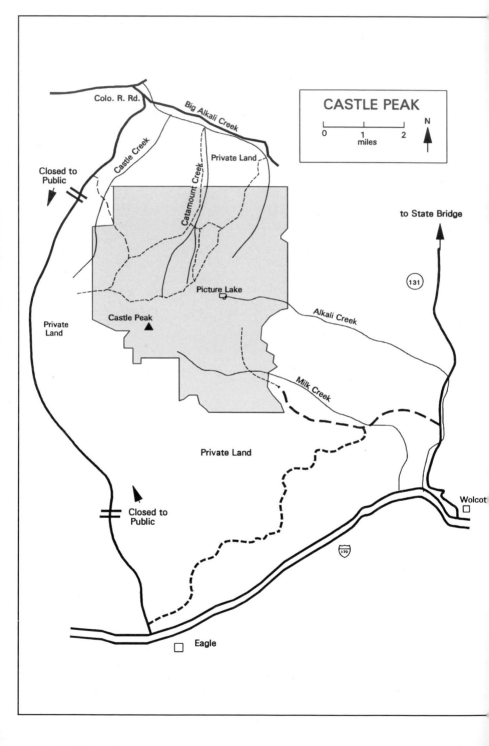

Castle Peak reflects on beaver pond, Castle Peak Wilderness Study Area. John Fielder photograph.

Castle Peak offers a delightful variety of hiking opportunities. Dense spruce-fir timber and chest-high grasses dominate the slopes north and west of the peak, and bushwhacking in these areas can be tiresome. The lower, and more accessible, eastern and southern slopes consist of rolling meadows crossed by several old vehicle ways that provide ready hiking routes to spectacular view points such as Picture Lake.

Castle Peak itself is not only a visual reference point for the whole area, but is interesting in its own right as an outlier of volcanic rock similar in age and origin to expanses of volcanic strata underlying the Flat Tops. Situated between the Flat Tops, Gore Range and Sawatch Range, Castle Peak provides sweeping vistas of much of Colorado's most dramatic mountain scenery. There is also good fishing for book trout in the area's many creeks and ponds.

Legal access to Castle Peak is best attained from the Milk Creek Road on the east side. Take state Highway 131 north from I-70 at the Wolcott exit. The Milk Creek Road, County Road 54, leaves Highway 131 in approximately three miles and winds its way onto the eastern slopes of the roadless area. Take the right branch of the road about 1.5 miles after leaving the highway. Leave the road where convenient and bushwhack toward one of the area's many small ponds or one of the overgrown four-wheel-drive trails. A four-wheel-drive vehicle is a must if the roads are wet.

BLM has recently purchased 80 acres in Section 31 on the northwest corner of the area to facilitate legal access. You reach this location from the north via the Colorado River road that runs between McCoy and Dotsero. About three miles east of Burns, turn south at the crest of Blue Hill where the road climbs high above the river canyon. Follow this road another three miles south, and take a left spur which leads to an obvious parking area. From here, hike along an obvious trail for a mile or so toward Winter Ridge, after which the trail fades away. Many old 'dozer trails criss-cross the forest on Winter Ridge and offer hiking routes.

From a map it may appear that a more direct route is found by taking the Eagle exit on I-70 and driving north, but this road is closed to the public four miles beyond its start.

39 DEEP CREEK

Location:	15 miles northeast of Glenwood Springs
Elevation Range:	6,200 – 10,460 feet
Vegetation/Ecosystem:	Piñon-juniper, aspen; spruce-fir
Roadless Acreage:	8,000 acres (includes 5,000 acres of Forest Service land)
Wilderness Status:	Not proposed for wilderness by BLM
Special Features:	Limestone canyon; numerous caves
USGS Maps:	Broken Rib Creek, Dotsero

Deep Creek carves an extremely rugged and remote limestone canyon and in the process creates one of Colorado's most pristine wilderness retreats. Beginning at Deep Lake near the Flat Tops Wilderness Area, Deep Creek plunges more than 4,500 feet in a span of only 15 miles before it reaches the Colorado River near Dotsero. The many extraordinary features of Deep Creek have prompted the BLM and Forest Service to evaluate the potential for protecting the canyon under the auspices of the Wild and Scenic Rivers Act.

The limestone strata of Deep Creek have created ideal conditions for the formation of caves, and Deep Creek is blessed with more than forty known caves. These include many of the state's most outstanding caves, including Groaning Cave, Colorado's longest at 10,000 feet; Big A Disappointment Cave, with the largest opening of any in the state; and 20-pound Tick Cave, still being explored and accessible only with scuba gear. These and many other caves in Deep Creek are described in Lloyd E. Paris's 1973 book, *The Caves of Colorado.*

The higher reaches of Deep Creek are covered with forests of aspen, spruce and fir, interspersed with grassy meadows. As the creek drops closer to its confluence with the Colorado River, the landscape becomes more arid and vegetation turns toward piñon-juniper and sagebrush. The combination of dense vegetation and rugged terrain creates ideal hiding habitat for black bear, elk and mountain lions.

There are a few faint trails in the area, but the primary route for those wishing to explore the length of Deep Creek is the streambed itself. Hiking the upper end of Deep Creek is extremely arduous and in sections requires slithering down waterfalls, groping along cliffs and ducking under fallen logs.

Deep Creek is reached via the Dotsero exit on I-70 east of Glenwood Springs. Take the Colorado River road two miles north from Dotsero and turn west onto the Coffee Pot Road. A primitive trail drops into the creek at a picnic area at the first switchback, approximately two miles up the road. From here,

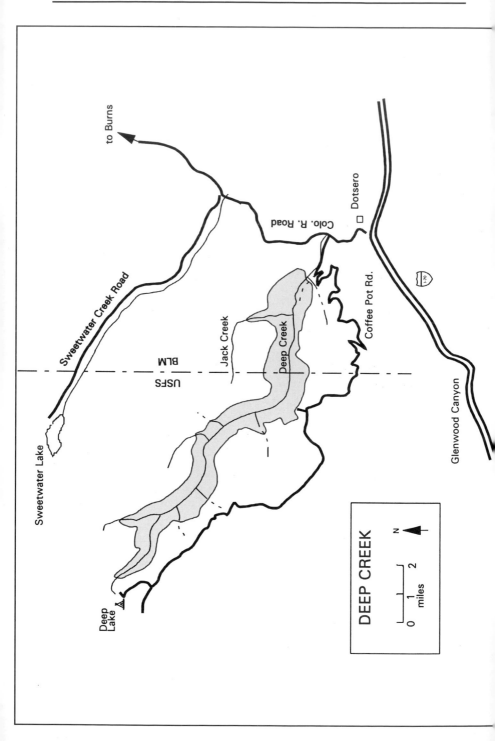

to Burns

Sweetwater Creek Road

Sweetwater Lake

Colo. R. Road

□ Dotsero

Coffee Pot Rd.

Jack Creek

USFS / BLM

Deep Creek

Glenwood Canyon

Deep Lake

DEEP CREEK

N

0   1   2
miles

it is possible more or less to easily follow the creek as it traverses BLM land for about three miles before entering the White River National Forest. The creek runs for another 10 miles through the National Forest to Deep Lake.

Several rough trails lead from the Coffee Pot Road to the rim of Deep Creek between the picnic area and Deep Lake Campground.

Looking down Deep Creek toward the Colorado River. John Fielder photograph.

John Fielder

40   GRAPE CREEK

Location:	10 miles southwest of Canon City
Elevation Range:	6,400 – 9,500 feet
Vegetation/Ecosystem:	Piñon-juniper; cottonwood; ponderosa pine; aspen
Roadless Acreage:	39,900 acres (includes 18,000 acres of Forest Service land)
Wilderness Status:	Not proposed for wilderness by BLM
Special Features:	Grape Creek canyon; large perennial stream; large-diameter trees; scenic vistas
USGS Maps:	Rockvale, Royal Gorge (15')

Most of the canyons of Colorado's Front Range have been developed in one fashion or another during the last century. Highways, towns, mines and powerlines are found separately or in combination. Grape Creek remains an exception to this general rule. Though a narrow-gauge railroad traveled the canyon

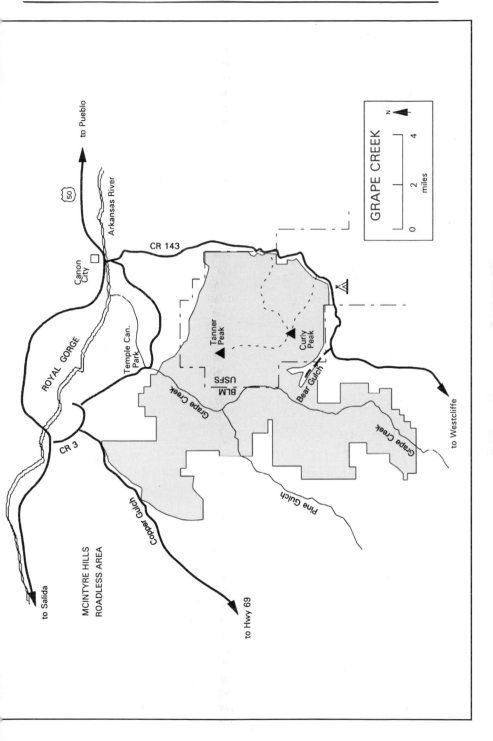

GRAPE CREEK

N

0 2 4
miles

to Pueblo

Arkansas River

50

Canon City

ROYAL GORGE

Temple Can. Park

CR 143

Tanner Peak

Curly Peak

BLM USFS

Grape Creek

Bear Gulch

to Westcliffe

Grape Creek

Pine Gulch

CR 3

Copper Gulch

to Salida

MCINTYRE HILLS ROADLESS AREA

to Hwy 69

in the 1880s, it has long since disappeared, and its bed now forms the basis of an easy hiking route.

The Grape Creek roadless area includes more than a dozen miles of Grape Creek and its lush riparian zone. Grape Creek has carved a rugged and scenic canyon through the metamorphic strata of the northern Wet Mountains. This canyon, which traverses the entire length of the roadless area, forms the primary travel route for hikers wishing to explore Grape Creek.

Life zones that range from the upper Sonoran to the montane offer a fascinating array of vegetative types, including sagebrush, rabbitbrush, cactus and yucca up through piñon-juniper woodland and into pine-spruce-fir forest intermixed with montane meadows and aspen at the highest elevations around Tanner Peak.

Predator populations, including high concentrations of mountain lions, indicate an abundance of prey species. Deer, elk, black bear and many smaller mammals are found here, as are wild turkeys. The expansive cliffs house nesting and roosting birds of prey, including eagles. The Colorado Division of Wildlife has identified possible nesting sites for the endangered peregrine falcon. Grape Creek is a large perennial stream that supports a significant brown and rainbow trout fishery.

The Grape Creek roadless area actually consists of three distinct administrative units: the BLM's Upper and Lower Grape Creek Wilderness Study Areas, separated by an off-road-vehicle trail in East Pierce Gulch and the 18,000-acre San Isabel National Forest Tanner Peak roadless area, which is contiguous to the eastern edge of Lower Grape Creek. The combination of units creates a diversity of recreational opportunities that range from canyon hiking to ascents of 9,500-foot peaks in the Wet Mountains.

Hikes into the mouth of Grape Creek begin at Temple Canyon City Park. Turn south on Fremont County Road 3 about 10 miles west of Canon City (this is also the road to the south entrance of the Royal Gorge). Follow the county road approximately seven miles to Temple Canyon City Park. Leave your vehicle at the park and follow the creek or the abandoned railroad grade upstream as far as you like. It is about 12 miles to the upper end of the roadless area. Grape Creek lies downstream from DeWeese Reservoir and drains much of the Wet Mountain Valley, so hikers should be cautious and treat any water used for human consumption.

The higher-elevation portions of the area around Tanner Peak are reached via the Oak Creek Grade Road (Fremont County 143) in the San Isabel National Forest. To connect with this road, turn south from Highway 50 in Canon City at the 4th Street Viaduct and turn south again in Prospect Heights onto Fremont County 143. The Tanner Trail takes off about 11 miles down the road and heads in a westerly direction to Curley Peak (three miles) and Tanner Peak (eight miles). The trail climbs sharply up Bear Gulch past forest giants to a summit ridge. Grassy parks and a spacious forest of stately ponderosa pine, aspen and fir trees define the ridge. Curley and Tanner peaks are rocky outcrops that provide sweeping views of the Sangre de Cristos and Pikes Peak and into Grape Creek Canyon.

A second Forest Service trail accesses Tanner Peak. The Stultz Trail also begins from Fremont County 143, about three miles north of the Tanner Trail, and a fine eight-mile circuit hike is possible combining the two trails.

The middle of Grape Creek Canyon is also accessible from County Road 143. Follow the road west about three miles beyond the Tanner Peak trail head and turn north at a BLM sign announcing public access to Grape Creek via Bear Gulch. This road is closed to vehicular traffic at the point where it reaches the creek, about three miles beyond County Road 143. There is easy hiking upstream or downstream along Grape Creek from this point.

Grape Creek winds its way through the Wet Mountains, Lower Grape Creek Wilderness Study Area. John Fielder photograph.

John Fielder

41   HACK LAKE

Location:	20 miles northeast of Glenwood Springs
Elevation Range:	7,600 – 11,000 feet
Vegetation/Ecosystem:	Transition from piñon-juniper to aspen and spruce-fir
Roadless Acreage:	9,120 acres (includes 6,000 acres of Forest Service land)
Wilderness Status:	10 acres proposed for wilderness by BLM
Special Features:	Ecological transition; access to Flat Tops Wilderness; spectacular vistas
USGS Maps:	Sweetwater Lake

The Flat Tops Wilderness is one of Colorado's most distinctive wilderness areas. It encompasses the vast expanse of the White River Plateau and is characterized by undulating tundra broken by pockets of spruce-fir forests and sparkling lakes tucked at the bases of volcanic cliffs.

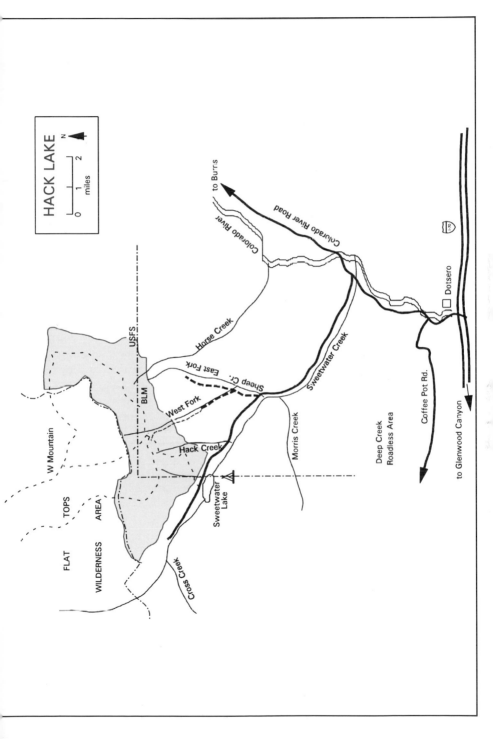

Hack Lake lies on the southern edge of the Flat Tops and offers hikers a dramatic approach to the wilderness. One major, well-maintained trail (the Ute Trail) traverses the Hack Lake Wilderness Study Area and eventually joins with the network of forest trails that lace the Flat Tops.

The lower elevations, and southern exposures, of Hack Lake are covered by a sparse piñon-juniper forest typical of the Colorado Plateau but surprising amid the lush forests of the Flat Tops. The Ute Trail winds across these exposed slopes, providing dramatic views of the Sawatch Range, and eventually turns the corner of the ridge to unveil an abrupt transition to groves of cool aspen with lush undergrowth. The trail splits just before reaching the bench on which Hack Lake itself sits, and the right branch goes on to connect with the W Mountain trail that crosses the Flat Tops.

Hack Creek pours out of a hillside, draining underground from Hack Lake on the shelf above. As the path tops out onto this bench area, it enters a spruce-fir forest that opens shortly to reveal the blue-green mirror of the small lake. Hack Lake is a spring-fed pond that no stream enters or leaves. Beyond, across a mountain meadow, graced by a picturesque and historic log cabin, the forest rolls up to summit cliffs. With each gain in elevation, the view unfolds a greater panorama, taking in the Gore Range and the Northern Sawatch to the east and the massive peaks of the Elk Range to the south.

To get to Hack Lake, follow the Colorado River road north from I-70 at Dotsero approximately six miles to the Sweetwater Lake Road. The Ute Trail begins immediately across the road from the Sweetwater Lake Resort (ask at the lodge if you can't find it) and is so named because it was an historic route of the Ute Indians. Several outfitters around Sweetwater Lake offer guided pack horse trips to Hack Lake.

A rougher, more remote approach to Hack Lake is via the four-wheel-drive trail in Sheep Creek. Turn north onto the four-wheel-drive road approximately eight miles up the Sweetwater Lake Road from the Colorado River. The road heads toward Dotsero State Wildlife Area. Take the left branch, and follow the road to its end — about 3.5 to four miles. From there, a trail leads several miles up Sheep Creek until it eventually connects with the Ute Trail and W Mountain Trail. The vegetation is rolling sagebrush-filled meadows that give way to aspen and spruce-fir.

John Fielder

42 MCINTYRE HILLS

Location:	12 miles west of Canon City
Elevation Range:	5,900 – 8,100 feet
Vegetation/Ecosystem:	Piñon-juniper; ponderosa pine; Douglas-fir
Roadless Acreage:	16,800 acres
Wilderness Status:	Not proposed for wilderness by BLM
Special Features:	Scenic vistas; rugged topography
USGS Maps:	Cotopaxi (15'), Royal Gorge (15')

Rolling, piñon-juniper–forested hills and steep rugged drainages range upward to the 8,100-foot elevation of the McIntyre Hills along the south bank of the Arkansas River. Ponderosa pine and Douglas-fir occur at higher elevations, and springs and pools in the major drainages provide a fairly reliable water source for wildlife and recreation.

Rugged topography and dense vegetation combine for excellent habitat for mule deer, black bear, turkey and small mammals. Golden eagles and prairie falcons nest here, and the area represents a sizable portion of the range of

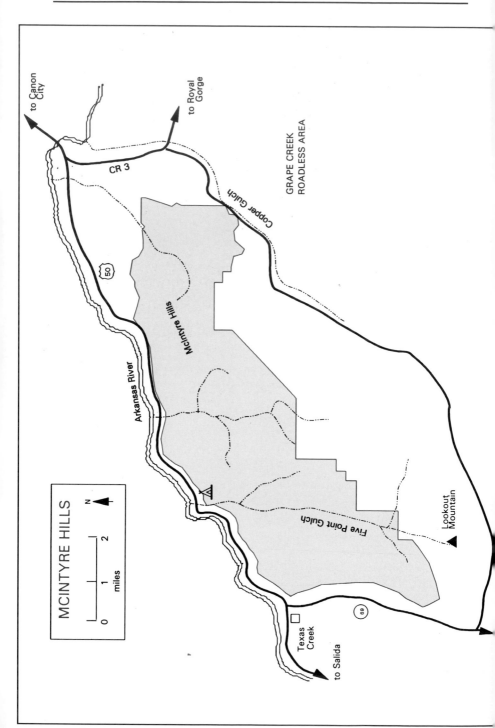

MCINTYRE HILLS

N

0   1   2
miles

to Canon City

to Royal Gorge

CR 3

50

Arkansas River

McIntyre Hills

Copper Gulch

GRAPE CREEK ROADLESS AREA

Five Point Gulch

Lookout Mountain

Texas Creek

69

to Salida

one of the densest populations of mountain lions in the western United States. McIntyre Hills is also a top priority of the Colorado Division of Wildlife for transplanting bighorn sheep.

McIntyre Hills is generally snow free and thus offers year-round hiking opportunities for the numerous residents of the nearby Front Range. Those visitors are assured almost total solitude by the lack of trails and the extremely rugged topography. The most immediate access to McIntyre Hills is from U.S. Highway 50. The roadless area begins along the highway approximately 2.5 miles east of Texas Creek and the junction with state Highway 69. From this point for another seven miles, the highway forms the area's northern boundary. Short, steep hikes up one of the gulches or directly to the ridge are possible in infinite combination, and the adjacent highway offers many possibilities for one-way hikes with car shuttles. For instance, you can scale the McIntyre Hills themselves at the eastern end of the roadless area and traverse the crest of the ridge for a couple of miles before dropping back to the highway. From the ridge crest, wave after wave of wild broken country unfolds, offering uncommon views of the Arkansas River gorge and the length of the Sangre de Cristo range.

Five Points Gulch is the longest drainage, stretching almost five miles into the heart of the roadless area. The drainage intersects Highway 50 approximately four miles east of Texas Creek, and hikes begin at the Colorado State Parks Five Points Recreation Site. The stream course is lined by giant cottonwoods, and the many rocky outcrops that dot adjacent ridges give vantage points for scanning jumbled terrain for new routes into seemingly unexplored tributaries. Exploring Five Points Gulch will undoubtedly result in a good day's exercise.

John Fielder

43   RIO GRANDE

Location:	10 miles east of Antonito
Elevation Range:	7,000 – 8,700 feet
Vegetation/Ecosystem:	Rabbitbrush; piñon-juniper
Roadless Acreage:	26,440 acres
Wilderness Status:	Not proposed for wilderness by BLM
Special Features:	Rio Grande; raptors; scenic vistas
USGS Maps:	Kiowa Hill, La Segita Peaks NE, Sky Valley Ranch, Ute Mountain

The most dramatic feature of this area is approximately eight miles of the Rio Grande river corridor. This segment of the river has been recommended by BLM for inclusion in the National Wild and Scenic Rivers system because of its remarkable raptor population and outstanding recreational opportunities. The river cuts a steep-sided canyon lined with riparian vegetation. The cliffs and the adjacent food source from the river draw raptors by the hundreds, among them hawks, falcons and eagles. The bald eagle, for example, is a common winter resident of the area, and as many as 300 bald eagles have

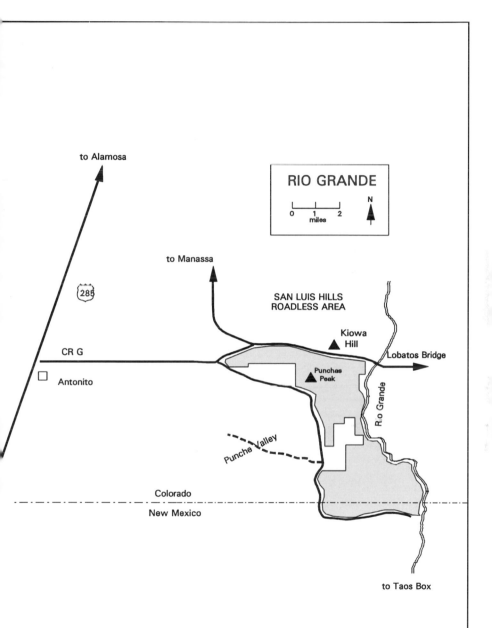

to Alamosa

RIO GRANDE

0   1   2
miles

N

to Manassa

SAN LUIS HILLS
ROADLESS AREA

285

CR G

Kiowa
Hill

Lobatos Bridge

Antonito

Punchas
Peak

Rio Grande

Punche Valley

Colorado

New Mexico

to Taos Box

been counted during a winter.

Recreational activities include floatboating, raptor viewing, fishing, hiking, camping and general wilderness solitude experiences. BLM estimates that approximately 500 float trips are taken annually from the Lobatos bridge south into New Mexico. Because of these attributes, BLM has designated this stretch of river as part of the longer Rio Grande River Corridor Special Recreation Management Area.

The area west of the river consists of an interesting and varied landscape of vast desert grasslands intersected by hills and ridges. Dominant vegetation types include western wheatgrass, Indian ricegrass, saltbrush and rabbitbrush.

Elevation within the proposed Rio Grande Wilderness ranges from 7,000 feet along the river to 8,700 feet on the highest point in the area, Punchas Peak. Vantage points such as this offer spectacular panoramic views of the San Luis Valley, the Rio Grande river corridor, the Sangre de Cristo range, the San Juan Mountains and two impressive landmarks known as the Twin Peaks–Ute Mountain and San Antonio Peak.

Rio Grande offers year-round habitat for pronghorn and mule deer. The Colorado Natural Areas Program has conducted field studies of the area looking for the rare and endangered plant species, *Astragalus ripleyi* (Ripley's milkvetch), which is known to inhabit rocky outcroppings and side canyons.

From Antonito, head east on the Kiowa Hill Road (County Road G) to a fork approximately nine miles out of town. The north fork defines the northern boundary of the roadless area and skirts several low hills. To climb Punchas Peak, park along the road three or four miles beyond the fork and head south cross-country a mile or two to the top of the hill. Continuing a couple of miles farther along this road takes you to the Lobatos bridge and an access point for Rio Grande float trips along the area's eastern edge.

Floating the river provides the best chance for glimpsing some of the numerous raptors in the area. The float is a flat-water trip suitable for any kind of watercraft if you take out before reaching the Taos Box. This requires an arduous climb with your craft out of the canyon, however. Continuing downstream, you will run into the wild whitewater of the Taos Box. Contact the BLM's Taos Resource Area office in New Mexico for more information about floating the Rio Grande.

The south fork takes you down the Punche Valley Road and provides access to the western side of the area. About four miles from the fork, the road bends south. It is a short mile hike to the top of Punchas Peak from this point or a two-mile hike east to the rim of the river canyon.

John Fielder

44 SAN LUIS HILLS

Location:	25 miles south of Alamosa
Elevation Range:	7,700 –9,300 feet
Vegetation/Ecosystem:	Fescue and mountain muhlyprairie; piñon-Juniper
Roadless Acreage:	20,000 acres
Wilderness Status:	Not proposed for wilderness by BLM
Special Features:	Scenic vistas; high desert biome
USGS Maps:	Kiowa, Manassa, Manassa NE

The San Luis Hills are a prominent and geologically unique landform of the southern San Luis Valley. Rising more than 1,000 feet above the valley floor, the San Luis Hills are an erosional remnant of the vast volcanic deposits that form the San Juan Mountains and underlie the soils of the valley. The area remained stable while the surrounding basin subsided along the faults of the Rio Grande Rift. The eastern flank of the area is the western fault along which the subsidence occurred, forming the present day Rio Grande river valley.

The volcanic layers underlying the San Luis Hills may be seen in steep rock

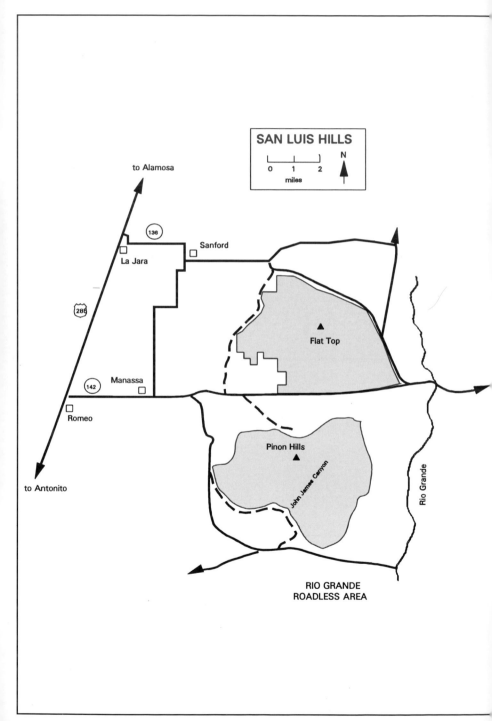

SAN LUIS HILLS

0 1 2
miles

N

to Alamosa

136

Sanford

La Jara

285

Manassa

142

Romeo

to Antonito

Flat Top

Pinon Hills

John James Canyon

Rio Grande

RIO GRANDE
ROADLESS AREA

Rabbitbrush shines above the Rio Grande, San Luis Hills Wilderness Study Area in distance. John Fielder photograph.

faces on the area's northern side. The area is dominated by rolling hills cut by twisting canyons, the longest of which is John James Canyon. Sweeping vistas of the San Luis Valley and surrounding mountain ranges are afforded from the unnamed summits in the area. This bird's-eye view provides a perspective of the river systems and landforms of the valley found nowhere else.

Wildlife species that inhabit the San Luis Hills include deer, pronghorn, various small mammal and rodent species, piñon jay and raptors. Water limits deer populations, as there are no perennial streams within the area. However, the San Luis Hills provide important coniferous cover and winter range to deer and antelope amid the agricultural lands of Conejos County.

Fall, winter and spring are the best times to visit the San Luis Hills. At a time when foothill areas at equal elevation may be snowed in, the physical isolation and southern exposure of the San Luis Hills combine to provide ideal conditions for winter hiking and horseback riding. Scattered archaeological sites, geologic features and potential raptor sightings are of particular interest to visitors. There are no water sources, so bring your own.

The San Luis Hills consist of two units separated by Highway 142. The southern unit goes by BLM's name for the wilderness study area, San Luis Hills; the northern unit is called Flat Top Mesa.

To reach San Luis Hills, travel south from Alamosa on U.S. Highway 285 and turn east on Highway 142. Approximately four miles east of Manassa, a couple of dirt roads head south from the highway to the northern edge of the San Luis Hills. Park anywhere along the dirt road that forms the area's northern boundary and pick a route.through the open sagebrush and scattered piñon-juniper 1,500 feet to the crest of the hills.

The southern side of San Luis Hills and the main drainage, John James Canyon, are also accessed via Highway 142. Turn south two miles east of Manassa and follow the network of roads that angles southeast toward the Rio Grande. John James Canyon slices to the heart of the roadless area, and a good loop hike is to follow the canyon to its head, scramble up the high hill to the west for views of the Sangre de Cristo range and the Rio Grande and then head south down the hillside a couple of miles back to your vehicle.

Flat Top Mesa lies directly across state Highway 142 north of San Luis Hills. The mesa top itself is unexpectedly vast, the rolling terrain hiding visitors from one another. A desert grassland, underlain by volcanic soil and rock, is populated by sweet-smelling sagebrush interspersed with blooming pricklypear cactus. A dirt track heads northeast toward Flat Top Mesa approximately six miles east of Manassa on the highway. Park along this track and hike a couple of miles cross-country through sagebrush and piñon-juniper to the mesa, which offers extraordinary views of the San Luis Valley and its environs. The Fairy Hills, Piñon Hills, Rio Grande, Sangre de Cristo Range, Great Sand Dunes and the San Juan Mountains complete a sweeping 360-degree vista.

The eastern and northern boundaries of the Flat Top Mesa roadless area are defined by a dirt road that angles northwest from Highway 142, approximately 10 miles east of Manassa and one mile west of the Rio Grande. Park anywhere along this road and strike out across about a mile of sagebrush flats to the base of the mesa, from which it is a short climb to the top.

Kirk Koepsel

45 THOMPSON CREEK

Location:	20 miles south of Glenwood Springs
Elevation Range:	6,600 – 10,700 feet
Vegetation/Ecosystem:	Cottonwood; oakbrush; piñon-juniper; Douglas-fir; aspen; ponderosa pine
Roadless Acreage:	23,200 acres (includes 16,000 acres of Forest Service land)
Wilderness Status:	Not proposed for wilderness by BLM
Special Features:	Rock formations; riparian zone
USGS Maps:	Mount Sopris, Placita, Redstone, Stony Ridge

Thompson Canyon is a Western Slope "Garden of the Gods." It contains the same geologic strata and vertical faulted hogbacks as those of the Colorado Springs phenomenon. Many of these jumbled red sediments parallel the Crystal River and are found on Assignation Ridge in adjacent National Forest lands.

Thompson Creek itself is a beautiful stream with undisturbed woods ranging from cottonwoods and ponderosa pine to scrub oak, piñon-juniper, Douglas-fir

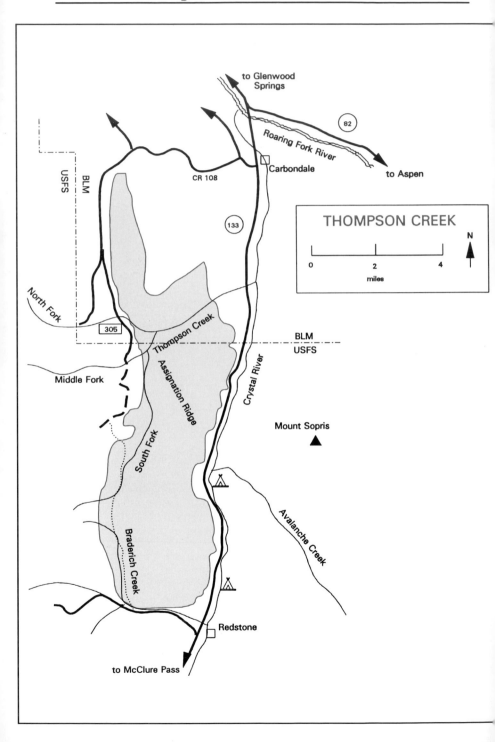

and aspen. It creates a haven for wildlife such as elk, bear, mountain lion and wild turkey in addition to the ubiquitous mule deer.

BLM has long recognized the beauty of the area, designating it an Area of Critical Environmental Concern. Thompson Creek is also under consideration as a possible Wild or Scenic addition to the potential Wild and Scenic River designation of the Crystal River.

Thompson Creek joins the Crystal River about 4.5 miles south of Carbondale along Highway 133, but the mouth of the canyon at this point is on private land and public access is effectively blocked by No Trespassing signs. It is best to drop into Thompson Creek from BLM land to the west. From Highway 133 in Carbondale, turn west onto Main Street, (Road 106) and follow it until it turns into Thompson Creek Road, (Road 108). In approximately seven miles, Forest Road 305 will branch left. This road crosses Thompson Creek in another two miles, at which point you can hike downstream into the roadless area. Remnants of trestles and the long-abandoned grade of the Aspen and Western Railroad are found in the lower canyon. The railway grade and the Thompson Creek streambed provide a track for hikers and cross-country skiers that is unequaled for spectacular scenery.

The southern end of the area, and the South Thompson Creek drainage, are most easily reached from the Braderich Trail on the White River National Forest. The Braderich Trail begins approximately 2.5 miles west of Redstone on the road to the Mid-Continent Resources coal mine. The trail heads up Braderich Creek for about three miles, crosses a saddle and drops into the headwaters of South Thompson Creek before cutting across the drainage basin and connecting with Forest Road 305. Exploring the creek will require leaving the trail for cross-country travel and bushwhacking along the creek banks.

John Fielder

46   TROUBLESOME

Location:	20 miles north of Kremmling
Elevation Range:	8,100 – 11,100 feet
Vegetation/Ecosystem:	Lodgepole pine; aspen; spruce-fir
Roadless Acreage:	87,450 acres (includes 75,000 acres of Forest Service land)
Wilderness Status:	Not proposed for wilderness by BLM
Special Features:	Forest streams; scenic views; big game
USGS Maps:	Hyannis Peak, Kremmling (15')

The Troublesome area contains the few relatively undisturbed valleys of the Middle Park region, including one of the lowest-elevation portions of the Continental Divide in Colorado. As a consequence of its lower elevations, Troublesome provides a contrast to existing designated wildernesses in the vicinity, which generally include high rugged peaks and steep, glaciated valleys. Troublesome possesses thick timber stands, aspen groves, grassy meadows, ample water and otherwise undisturbed conditions that provide excellent habitat for a wide variety of wildlife species. Mule deer, elk, bobcat, bear,

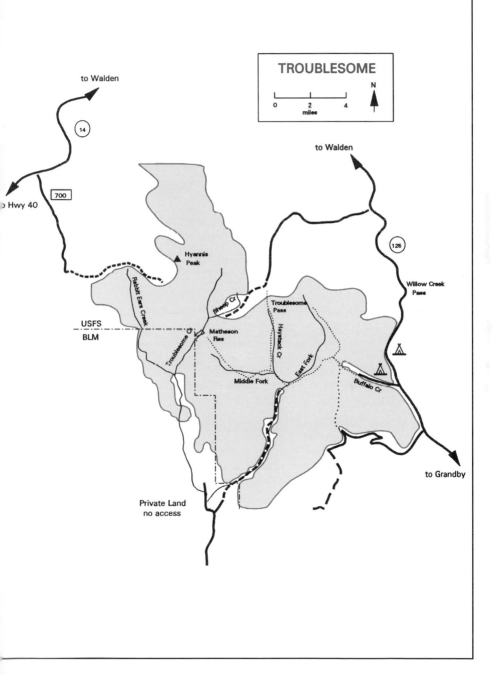

golden eagles and prairie falcons are among the most notable inhabitants. Bald eagles summer in the area, and peregrine falcons have been sighted here also.

Troublesome is a combined BLM/Forest Service roadless area, with the BLM portion containing only about 10,000 of the 87,000 acres in the area. The BLM segment, however, includes important low-elevation riparian zones along Troublesome Creek and Rabbit Ears Creek in the southwest corner of the area.

The largest deer and elk herds in Middle and North parks calve, summer and winter within Troublesome. There is potential for moose to move into the area from recent North Park transplants. The Colorado Division of Wildlife believes that the area must remain in its undeveloped state to maintain the existing elk populations in Middle Park.

Over 50 miles of trails provide for a variety of dispersed recreational activity, including hiking, horseback riding, backpacking, ski touring, fishing, hunting and nature study. Unfortunately, private land blocks direct access from nearby roads to the BLM portion of Troublesome. It is possible to get into the BLM area either by traveling cross-country or in a roundabout fashion using existing Forest Service trails.

The headwaters of Rabbit Ears Creek are reached via Forest Road 700, which leaves the east side of Highway 14 halfway between Walden and Muddy Pass. From this road, follow a four-wheel-drive road east along the Continental Divide toward an electronic site and after a couple of miles drop into the Rabbit Ears Creek drainage. No trails exist in this drainage, so you are on your own as far as route finding is concerned. The creek crosses into the BLM area about four miles downstream. Cross-country travel down Sheep Creek or Poison Creek from the network of logging roads north of Troublesome Pass will also take you into the BLM area.

Forest Service trails on East Fork, Middle Fork Creek, and Haystack Creek can be used to reach Troublesome Creek on BLM land. Take Highway 125 north from Windy Gap to Buffalo Creek and turn left several miles to the end of the public road. A Forest Service trail heads west from here into the East Fork. Upon reaching the creek, head west and in several miles take Forest Trail 57 up Middle Fork Creek. This trail ultimately leads to Matheson Reservoir, which sits on Troublesome Creek at the BLM/Forest Service boundary. The Haystack Creek trail (Forest Trail 55) also connects with Middle Fork Creek but enters from the north over Troublesome Pass instead of from the east.

SELECTED REFERENCES

For more information about various topics mentioned in this book, particularly with regard to natural history, and for additional sources of route descriptions for some areas, the following list of selected titles is recommended.

Boddie, Caryn and Peter. *The Hiker's Guide to Colorado*. Helena, Montana: Falcon Press Publishing Co., 1991. 301 p.

Borneman, Walter R. and Lyndon J. Lampert, *A Climbing Guide to Colorado's Fourteeners*. Boulder, Colorado. Pruett Publishing Co., 1990. 255 p.

Cassells, E. Steve. *The Archaeology of Colorado*. Boulder, Colorado: Johnson Books, 1990. 325 p.

Chronic, Halka. *Roadside Geology of Colorado*. Missoula, Montana: Mountain Press Publishing Co., 1980. 335 p.

Cockrell, David. *The Wilderness Educator: The Wilderness Education Association Curriculum Guide*. Merrillville, Indiana: ICS Books, 1991. 194 p.

Kelsey, Michael R. *Canyon Hiking Guide to the Colorado Plateau*. Provo, Utah: Kelsey Publishing, 1991. 288 p.

Ormes, Robert M. *Guide to the Colorado Mountains*. Colorado Springs, Colorado: Robert M. Ormes, 1983. 356 p.

Paris, Lloyd E. *Caves of Colorado*. Boulder, Colorado: Pruett Publishing Co., 1973. 247 p.

Simer, Peter and John Sullivan. *The National Outdoor Leadership School's Wilderness Guide*. New York: Simon and Schuster, 1983. 345 p.

Wheat, Doug. *The Floater's Guide to Colorado*. Helena, Montana: Falcon Press Publishing Co., 1983. 296 p.

Zwinger, Ann. *Run, River, Run*. Tucson, Arizona: The University of Arizona Press, 1975. 317 p.

Zwinger, Ann. *Wind in the Rock*. Tucson, Arizona: The University of Arizona Press, 1978. 258 p.

APPENDIX A

BLM OFFICES

COLORADO STATE OFFICE
2850 Youngfield Street
Lakewood, Colorado 80215
(303) 239-3600

CANON CITY DISTRICT

Royal Gorge Resource Area
3170 East Main Street
P.O. Box 2200
Canon City, Colorado 81215-2200
(719) 275-0631

San Luis Resource Area
1921 State Street
Alamosa, Colorado 81101
(719) 589-4975

CRAIG DISTRICT

Kremmling Resource Area
1116 Park Avenue
P.O. Box 68
Kremmling, Colorado 80459
(303) 724-3437

Little Snake Resource Area
1280 Industrial Avenue
Craig, Colorado 81625
(303) 824-4441

White River Resource Area
P.O. Box 928
Meeker, Colorado 81641
(303) 878-3601

GRAND JUNCTION DISTRICT

Grand Junction Resource Area
764 Horizon Drive
Grand Junction, Colorado 81506
(303) 243-6561

Glenwood Springs Resource Area
50629 Highways 6 & 24
P.O. Box 1009
Glenwood Springs, Colorado 81602
(303) 945-2341

MONTROSE DISTRICT

Gunnison Resource Area
216 North Colorado
Gunnison, Colorado 81230
(303) 641-0471

San Juan Resource Area
Federal Building
701 Camino del Rio
Durango, Colorado 81301
(303) 247-4082

Uncompahgre Basin Resource Area
2505 South Townsend Avenue
Montrose, Colorado 81401
(303) 249-7791

APPENDIX B

COLORADO CONSERVATION GROUPS WORKING ON BLM WILDERNESS ISSUES

Colorado Audubon Council
4150 Darley, #5
Boulder, CO 80303
(303) 499-0219

Colorado Environmental Coalition
777 Grant Street, Suite 606
Denver, Colorado 80203
(303) 837-8701

Colorado Mountain Club
2530 West Alameda Avenue
Denver, Colorado 80219
(303) 922-8315

Colorado Wildlife Federation
7475 Dakin Street
Westminster, Colorado 80210
(303) 429-4500

The Nature Conservancy
1244 Pine Street
Boulder, Colorado 80302
(303) 444-2950

Sierra Club, Rocky Mountain Chapter
777 Grant Street, Suite 606
Denver, Colorado 80203
(303) 861-8819

Sierra Club, Southwest Regional Office
1240 Pine Street
Boulder, Colorado 80302
(303) 449-5595

Trout Unlimited
655 Broadway, #475
Denver, Colorado 80203
(303) 595-0620

Western Colorado Congress
P.O. Box 472
Montrose, Colorado 81402
(303) 249-1978

The Wilderness Society
777 Grant Street, Suite 606
Denver, Colorado 80203
(303) 839-1175

INDEX

MARK PEARSON

Mark Pearson has been active in Colorado wilderness issues with the Sierra Club and Colorado Environmental Coalition for more than a decade. He first began exploring Colorado's BLM lands in 1978 with a hike into Demaree Canyon and has since become an avid proponent of desert wilderness in Colorado. Pearson participated as a citizen in the planning and management decisions for all of the areas described in this book and has personally visited all but one or two of them.

Pearson grew up in the Denver metropolitan area. After living in Grand Junction for the past nine years, he is currently pursuing a graduate degree in natural resource management at Colorado State University in Fort Collins, where he resides with his wife, Sherree Tatum.

JOHN FIELDER

John Fielder has been photographing the natural world since 1973. He is the photographer of 12 books, including eight about his adopted state of Colorado. His latest books, *Along the Colorado Trail* (May 1992) and *Colorado, Rivers of the Rockies* (June 1993), are available at all Colorado bookstores.

A former department store executive who transformed an avocation into a new career, Fielder is active in conservation issues, civic affairs, photography instruction and the publishing industry.

Fielder is also a devoted family man. Do not be surprised to see him on the trail with a string of llamas, a large camera case, his wife and a pack of kids. Fielder and his family live in Greenwood Village, Colorado.